THE FORGOTTEN PEOPLE

THE
FORGOTTEN PEOPLE

AND OTHER STUDIES IN DEMOCRACY

By

ROBERT GORDON MENZIES

ANGUS AND ROBERTSON LTD
SYDNEY :: LONDON
1943

Set up, printed and bound
in Australia by
Halstead Press Pty Limited
9-19 Nickson Street, Sydney
1943

Registered in Australia for
transmission through the
post as a book.

Republished edition 2017 by Connor Court Publishing
in conjunction with the Menzies Research Centre, Canberra.

Published under the imprint: Jeparit Press
A Connor Court imprint in association with the Menzies Research Centre
(Connor Court Publishing)
PO Box 7257
Redland Bay QLD 4165

www.connorcourt.com

ISBN: 978-1-925501-44-5

Scanning of the original book by Ian James

FOREWORD

The broadcast essays in this volume were delivered weekly during 1942. Some of them deal with matters of permanent interest while others are dated by passing events. They have represented a serious attempt to clarify my own mind and assist listeners on questions which emerge in the changing currents of war. In a sense, within the acute limits of time and space, they represent a summarized political philosophy to which many thousands have been interested enough to listen and which hundreds of listeners-in have asked me to publish.

It should perhaps be stated that their preparation and delivery have been a purely voluntary contribution on my part to the solution of contemporary problems. I am indebted to Station 2UE, Sydney, and its associated stations in Victoria and Queensland, for their courtesy in enabling this to be done; and to Messrs Robertson and Mullens Ltd of Melbourne for having published and circulated at their own cost the broadcast "The Forgotten People", which gives its name to this book.

CONTENTS

I

THE FORGOTTEN PEOPLE

QUITE recently, a bishop wrote a letter to a great daily newspaper. His theme was the importance of doing justice to the
workers. His belief, apparently, was that the workers are those
who work with their hands. He sought to divide the people
of Australia into classes. He was obviously suffering from what
has for years seemed to me to be our greatest political disease—
the disease of thinking that the community is divided into
the rich and relatively idle, and the laborious poor, and that
every social and political controversy can be resolved into the
question: What side are you on?

Now, the last thing that I want to do is to commence or
take part in a false war of this kind. In a country like Australia
the class war must always be a false war. But if we are to
talk of classes, then the time has come to say something of
the forgotten class—the middle class—those people who are
constantly in danger of being ground between the upper and
the nether millstones of the false class war; the middle class
who, properly regarded, represent the backbone of this country.

We do not have classes here as in England, and therefore
the terms do not mean the same; so I must define what I mean
when I use the expression "middle class".

Let me first define it by exclusion. I exclude at one end of the
scale the rich and powerful: those who control great funds and
enterprises, and are as a rule able to protect themselves—though
it must be said that in a political sense they have as a rule shown

neither comprehension nor competence. But I exclude them because, in most material difficulties, the rich can look after themselves.

I exclude at the other end of the scale the mass of unskilled people, almost invariably well-organized, and with their wages and conditions safeguarded by popular law. What I am excluding them from is my definition of the middle class. We cannot exclude them from the problem of social progress, for one of the prime objects of modern social and political policy is to give to them a proper measure of security, and provide the conditions which will enable them to acquire skill and knowledge and individuality.

These exclusions being made, I include the intervening range —the kind of people I myself represent in Parliament—salary-earners, shopkeepers, skilled artisans, professional men and women, farmers, and so on. These are, in the political and economic sense, the middle class. They are for the most part unorganized and unself-conscious. They are envied by those whose social benefits are largely obtained by taxing them. They are not rich enough to have individual power. They are taken for granted by each political party in turn. They are not sufficiently lacking in individualism to be organized for what in these days we call "pressure politics". And yet, as I have said, they are the backbone of the nation.

The communist has always hated what he calls the "bourgeoisie", because he sees clearly that the existence of one has kept British countries from revolution, while the substantial absence of one in feudal France at the end of the eighteenth century and in Tsarist Russia at the end of the last war made revolution easy and indeed inevitable.

You may say to me, "Why bring this matter up at this stage, when we are fighting a war in the result of which we are all equally concerned?" My answer is that I am bringing it up because under the pressures of war we may, if we are not careful —if we are not as thoughtful as the times will permit us to be—inflict a fatal injury upon our own backbone.

In point of political, industrial and social theory and practice there are great delays in time of war. But there are also great accelerations. We must watch each, remembering always that whether we know it or not, and whether we like it or not, the foundations of whatever new order is to come after the war are inevitably being laid down now. We cannot go wrong right up to the peace treaty and expect suddenly thereafter to go right.

Now, what is the value of this middle class, so defined and described? First, it has "a stake in the country". It has responsibility for homes—homes material, homes human, homes spiritual.

I do not believe that the real life of this nation is to be found either in great luxury hotels and the petty gossip of so-called fashionable suburbs, or in the officialdom of organized masses. It is to be found in the homes of people who are nameless and unadvertised, and who, whatever their individual religious conviction or dogma, see in their children their greatest contribution to the immortality of their race. The home is the foundation of sanity and sobriety; it is the indispensable condition of continuity; its health determines the health of society as a whole.

I have mentioned homes material, homes human, and homes spiritual. Let me take them in their order. What do I mean by "homes material"?

The material home represents the concrete expression of the habits of frugality and saving "for a home of our own". Your advanced socialist may rage against private property even while he acquires it; but one of the best instincts in us is that which induces us to have one little piece of earth with a house and a garden which is ours: to which we can withdraw, in which we can be among our friends, into which no stranger may come against our will.

If you consider it, you will see that if, as in the old saying, "the Englishman's home is his castle", it is this very fact that leads on to the conclusion that he who seeks to violate that law by violating the soil of England must be repelled and defeated.

National patriotism, in other words, inevitably springs from the instinct to defend and preserve our own homes.

Then we have homes human. A great house, full of loneliness, is not a home. "Stone walls do not a prison make", nor do they make a house. They may equally make a stable or a piggery. Brick walls, dormer windows and central heating need not make more than a hotel. My home is where my wife and children are. The instinct to be with them is the great instinct of civilized man; the instinct to give them a chance in life—to make them not leaners but lifters—is a noble instinct.

If Scotland has made a great contribution to the theory and practice of education, it is because of the tradition of Scottish homes. The Scottish ploughman, walking behind his team, cons ways and means of making his son a farmer, and so he sends him to the village school. The Scottish farmer ponders upon the future of his son, and sees it most assured not by the inheritance of money but by the acquisition of that knowledge which will give him power; and so the sons of many Scottish farmers find their way to Edinburgh and a university degree.

The great question is, "How can I qualify my son to help society?" Not, as we have so frequently thought, "How can I qualify society to help my son?" If human homes are to fulfil their destiny, then we must have frugality and saving for education and progress.

And finally, we have homes spiritual. This is a notion which finds its simplest and most moving expression in "The Cotter's Saturday Night" of Burns. Human nature is at its greatest when it combines dependence upon God with independence of man.

We offer no affront—on the contrary we have nothing but the warmest human compassion—toward those whom fate has compelled to live upon the bounty of the State, when we say that the greatest element in a strong people is a fierce independence of spirit. This is the only *real* freedom, and it has as its corollary a brave acceptance of unclouded individual responsibility. The moment a man seeks moral and intellectual refuge in the emotions of a crowd, he ceases to be a human being and becomes a cipher. The home spiritual so understood is not produced by lassitude or by dependence; it is produced by self-sacrifice, by frugality and saving.

In a war, as indeed at most times, we become the ready victims of phrases. We speak glibly of many things without pausing to consider what they signify. We speak of "financial power", forgetting that the financial power of 1942 is based upon the savings of generations which have preceded it. We speak of "morale" as if it were a quality induced from without—created by others for our benefit—when in truth there can be no national morale which is not based upon the individual courage of men and women. We speak of "man power" as if it were a mere matter of arithmetic: as if it were made up of a multiplication of men and muscles without spirit.

Second, the middle class, more than any other, provides the intelligent ambition which is the motive power of human progress. The idea entertained by many people that, in a well-constituted world, we shall all live on the State is the quintessence of madness, for what is the State but *us?* We collectively must provide what we individually receive.

The great vice of democracy—a vice which is exacting a bitter retribution from it at this moment—is that for a generation we have been busy getting ourselves on to the list of beneficiaries and removing ourselves from the list of contributors, as if somewhere there was somebody else's wealth and somebody else's effort on which we could thrive.

To discourage ambition, to envy success, to hate achieved superiority, to distrust independent thought, to sneer at and impute false motives to public service—these are the maladies of modern democracy, and of Australian democracy in particular. Yet ambition, effort, thinking, and readiness to serve are not only the design and objectives of self-government but are the essential conditions of its success. If this is not so, then we had better put back the clock, and search for a benevolent autocracy once more.

Where do we find these great elements most commonly? Among the defensive and comfortable rich, among the unthinking and unskilled mass, or among what I have called the "middle class"?

Third, the middle class provides more than perhaps any other the intellectual life which marks us off from the beast: the life which finds room for literature, for the arts, for science, for medicine and the law.

Consider the case of literature and art. Could these survive as a department of State? Are we to publish our poets according to their political colour? Is the State to decree surrealism because surrealism gets a heavy vote in a key electorate? The truth is that no great book was ever written and no great picture ever painted by the clock or according to civil service rules. These things are done by man, not men. You cannot regiment them.

They require opportunity, and sometimes leisure. The artist, if he is to live, must have a buyer; the writer an audience. He finds them among frugal people to whom the margin above bare living means a chance to reach out a little towards that heaven which is just beyond our grasp. It has always seemed to me, for example, that an artist is better helped by the man who sacrifices something to buy a picture he loves than by a rich patron who follows the fashion.

Fourth, this middle class maintains and fills the higher schools and universities, and so feeds the lamp of learning.

What are schools for? To train people for examinations, to enable people to comply with the law, or to produce developed men and women?

Are the universities mere technical schools, or have they as one of their functions the preservation of pure learning, bringing in its train not merely riches for the imagination but a comparative sense for the mind, and leading to what we need so badly—the recognition of values which are other than pecuniary?

One of the great blots on our modern living is the cult of false values, a repeated application of the test of money, notoriety, applause. A world in which a comedian or a beautiful half-wit on the screen can be paid fabulous sums, whilst scientific researchers and discoverers can suffer neglect and starvation, is a world which needs to have its sense of values violently set right.

Now, have we realized and recognized these things, or is most of our policy designed to discourage or penalize thrift, to encourage dependence on the State, to bring about a dull equality on the fantastic idea that all men are equal in mind and needs and deserts: to level down by taking the mountains out of the landscape, to weigh men according to their political organizations and power—as votes and not as human beings? These are

B

formidable questions, and we cannot escape from answering them if there is really to be a new order for the world.

I have been actively engaged in politics for fourteen years in the State of Victoria and in the Commonwealth of Australia. In that period I cannot readily recall many occasions upon which any policy was pursued which was designed to help the thrifty, to encourage independence, to recognize the divine and valuable variations of men's minds. On the contrary, there have been many instances in which the votes of the thriftless have been used to defeat the thrifty. On occasions of emergency, as in the depression and during the present war, we have hastened to make it clear that the provision made by man for his own retirement and old age is not half as sacrosanct as the provision the State would have made for him had he never saved at all.

We have talked of income from savings as if it possessed a somewhat discreditable character. We have taxed it more and more heavily. We have spoken slightingly of the earning of interest at the very moment when we have advocated new pensions and social schemes. I have myself heard a minister of power and influence declare that no deprivation is suffered by a man if he still has the means to fill his stomach, clothe his body and keep a roof over his head. And yet the truth is, as I have endeavoured to show, that frugal people who strive for and obtain the margin above these materially necessary things are the whole foundation of a really active and developing national life.

The case for the middle class is the case for a dynamic democracy as against a stagnant one. Stagnant waters are level, and in them the scum rises. Active waters are never level: they toss and tumble and have crests and troughs; but the scientists tell us that they purify themselves in a few hundred yards.

That we are all, as human souls, of like value cannot be

denied. That each of us should have his chance is and must be the great objective of political and social policy. But to say that the industrious and intelligent son of self-sacrificing and saving and forward-looking parents has the same social deserts and even material needs as the dull offspring of stupid and improvident parents is absurd.

If the motto is to be, "Eat, drink and be merry, for to-morrow you will die, and if it chances you don't die, the State will look after you; but if you don't eat, drink and be merry, and save, we shall take your savings from you", then the whole business of life will become foundationless.

Are you looking forward to a breed of men after the war who will have become boneless wonders? Leaners grow flabby; lifters grow muscles. Men without ambition readily become slaves. Indeed, there is much more slavery in Australia than most people imagine. How many hundreds of thousands of us are slaves to greed, to fear, to newspapers, to public opinion— represented by the accumulated views of our neighbours! Land-less men smell the vapours of the street corner. Landed men smell the brown earth, and plant their feet upon it and know that it is good.

To all of this many of my friends will retort, "Ah, that's all very well, but when this war is over the levellers will have won the day." My answer is that, on the contrary, men will come out of this war as gloriously unequal in many things as when they entered it. Much wealth will have been destroyed; inherited riches will be suspect; a fellowship of suffering, if we really experience it, will have opened many hearts and perhaps closed many mouths. Many great edifices will have fallen, and we shall be able to study foundations as never before, because war will have exposed them.

But I do not believe that we shall come out into the overlordship of an all-powerful State on whose benevolence we shall live, spineless and effortless—a State which will dole out bread and ideas with neatly regulated accuracy; where we shall all have our dividend without subscribing our capital; where the Government, that almost deity, will nurse us and rear us and maintain us and pension us and bury us; where we shall all be civil servants, and all presumably, since we are equal, heads of departments.

If the new world is to be a world of men, we must be not pallid and bloodless ghosts, but a community of people whose motto shall be, "To strive, to seek, to find, and not to yield". Individual enterprise must drive us forward. That does not mean that we are to return to the old and selfish notions of laissez-faire. The functions of the State will be much more than merely keeping the ring within which the competitors will fight. Our social and industrial obligations will be increased. There will be more law, not less; more control, not less.

But what really happens to us will depend on how many people we have who are of the great and sober and dynamic middle-class—the strivers, the planners, the ambitious ones. We shall destroy them at our peril.

22 May, 1942.

II

THE FOUR FREEDOMS

Speaking last year, President Roosevelt, in discussing the things at stake in this war, made use of an expression—"The Four Freedoms"—which has now found currency in most of our mouths. The four freedoms to which he referred were: freedom of speech and expression, freedom of worship, freedom from want, freedom from fear.

One has only to state them to get a response from the listener. Every one of us will at once say, "Ah yes, I believe in those freedoms. The President is right." That the President is right I have no doubt myself; but that we either fully understand or believe in these freedoms is open to some question.

I propose therefore, in this and my next few broadcasts, to take each of these four freedoms in turn, endeavour to get at its meaning and significance, and work out what it involves in our own living and thinking.

To-night, then, I take the first freedom—freedom of speech and expression—which connotes also freedom of thought. This is a magnificent ideal, but what does it mean?

Let us, on the threshold of our consideration, remember that the whole essence of freedom is that it is freedom for others as well as for ourselves: freedom for people who disagree with us as well as for our supporters; freedom for minorities as well as for majorities. Here we have a conception which is not born with us but which we must painfully acquire. Most of us have no instinct at all to preserve the right of the other fellow to think what he likes about our beliefs and say what he likes about our opinions. The more primitive the community the less freedom of thought and expression is it likely to concede.

All things considered, the worst crime of fascism and its twin brother, German national socialism, is their suppression of free thought and free speech. It is one of the many proofs that, with all their cleverness, they are primitive and reactionary movements. One of the first actions of the Nazis in Germany was to regiment the newspapers by telling them exactly what they could print. The result was that newspaper controversy came to an end, since all sang the same tune. When I was in Berlin in 1938 I mentioned this phenomenon to a high German official of the Foreign Office and, with about the one gleam of humour that I encountered on that visit, he replied that he thought it quite a good idea, since it saved buying more than one newspaper. As you probably know, I am one who has in recent years had a severe battering from many newspapers, but I am still shocked to think that intelligent men, in what they believe to be a free country, can deny to the newspapers or to critics of any degree the right to batter at people or policies whom they dislike or of whom they disapprove.

Now, why is this first freedom of real importance to humanity? The answer is that what appears to be to-day's truth is frequently to-morrow's error. There is nothing absolute about the truth. It is elusive. In the old phrase, "it lies at the bottom of a deep well". It is hard to come at. So few of us have objective minds— detached minds—and what we conceive to be the truth is very often coloured or distorted by our own passions or interests or prejudices. Hence, if truth is to emerge and in the long run be triumphant, the process of free debate—the untrammelled clash of opinion—must go on.

There are fascist tendencies in all countries—a sort of latent tyranny. And they exist, be it remembered, in radical as well as in conservative quarters. Suppression of attack, which is based upon suppression of really free thought, is the instinctive weapon of the vested interest. And vested interests are not all one way. We have, for example, waged a fairly successful war against profit-making vested interests in the last two or three years; the war has placed an almost crushing burden upon them. But it would be indeed a casual observer who failed to notice that the vested interests of the great trade unions are growing. All these interests must remember—and so must we who are ordinary members of the public—that great groups which feel their power are at once subject to tremendous temptations to use that power so as to limit the freedom of others.

Many of you will recall John Stuart Mill's famous essay on Liberty, which was published eighty-three years ago, but is still full of freshness and truth. In the course of that essay Mill stated many principles, four of which I should like to put to you in his own words. First:

There is a limit to the legitimate interference of collective opinion with individual independence: and to find that limit, and maintain it against encroachment, is as indispensable to a good condition of human affairs as protection against political despotism.

What is being pointed to in that passage is the easily forgotten truth that the despotism of a majority may be just as bad as the despotism of one man. Public opinion in a reasonably educated community will, I believe, in the long run over a term of years, tend to be sound and just; but public day-to-day opinion, which must frequently be ill-informed, is quite capable of being not only wrong, but so extravagant as to be unjust and oppressive.

My second passage from Mill is this:

The principle is, that the sole end for which mankind are warranted, individually or collectively, in interfering with the liberty of action of any of their number is self-protection. That the only purpose for which power can be rightfully exercised over any member of a civilized community, against his will, is to prevent harm to others.

Here again we have a pregnant truth. It is a good rule, not only of common law but of social morality, that we must so use our own as not to injure others. The man who claims too much aggressive liberty for himself may be getting it at the expense of somebody else. Liberty is for all, not for some.

Mill next says:

As the tendency of all the changes taking place in the world is to strengthen society and diminish the power of the individual, this encroachment is not one of the evils which tend spontaneously to disappear, but, on the contrary, to grow more and more formidable.

I find this passage particularly illuminating. Fascism and the Nazi movement are both based upon a social philosophy which elevates the all-powerful State and makes the rights of the individual, not matters of inherent dignity but matters merely of concession by the State. Each says to the ordinary citizen, "Your rights are not those you were born with, but those which of our kindness we allow you." It is good to be reminded by Mill that this tendency is not confined to any one country. As the organization of society becomes more complex we must be increasingly vigilant for the freedom of our minds and spirits.

My final passage from Mill is this:

Complete liberty of contradicting and disproving our opinion is the very condition which justifies us in assuming its truth for purposes of action; and on no other terms can a being with human faculties have any rational assurance of being right.

In other words, it is a poorly founded and weakly held belief which cannot resist the onset of another man's critical mind.

There are, without doubt, limits on all these matters in time of war. When the battle is on, when nations are in a death struggle with other nations, the supremacy of the national security is clear and undoubted. That is the whole justification for war-time censorship, as well as the element that sets limits to it.

But even in time of war we must watch these things. You will agree that I speak as one with some practical—and occasion-ally painful—experience, when I say that the arrow of the critic is never pleasant and is sometimes poisoned. Much criticism is acutely partisan or actually unjust. But every man engaged in public affairs must sustain it with a good courage and a cheerful heart. He may, if he can, confute his critic, but he must not suppress him. Power is apt to produce a kind of drunkenness, and it needs the cold douche of the critic to correct it.

There are, at times like these, temptations towards political censorship or, what is just as bad, politically conscious censor-ship. The temptation towards suppression of thought and speech is greatest of all in time of war because at such a time people say, "Let us have strength!"—all too frequently meaning, by "strength", suppression; whereas the truth is that it requires more strength of character to sustain adverse or bitter criticism than to say, with a grand gesture, "Off with the critic's head!"

We are, if we take thought about them, conscious of certain facts. It requires great moral courage to put an unpopular view in Parliament or on the platform; to speak and vote against a popular but foolish strike at a union meeting; to denounce social evils amid the disturbed and relaxed social conditions and standards of war.

All these things are proof that we are as yet far short of really understanding or practising President Roosevelt's first freedom.

In a few minutes one can do little more than indicate the nature of the problem. But it is clear that it gives us much food for thought and self-examination.

Of all the countries I have visited, England is the one where freedom of thought and expression is best understood. And that fact has given to the English people a wide tolerance of opinion and a quiet wisdom of understanding that we have yet to achieve.

19 June, 1942.

III

THE FOUR FREEDOMS

Freedom of Speech and Expression (*Continued*)

Last week when I spoke to you of the first of President Roosevelt's four freedoms—freedom of speech, I had intended to deal this week with the second freedom—freedom of worship. But the programme must, I think, be altered, for last week's broadcast, in which the theme was the importance to democratic civilization of free criticism, was interpreted in some quarters as a special plea for some special kind of freedom for the Press. Now, I believe in a free Press, and in no way undervalue its importance; but I do not believe in a privileged Press.

There is something to be said for the view that in a democracy the eternal and real conflict is between freedom for all and privilege for some. Let me take your time to-night in explaining what I mean by that.

The Press of Australia, very naturally, devotes a good deal of space to discussing public men. They will, I am sure, have no objection to the process being, for once, courteously reversed.

I have never been able to accept the idea that newspapers have some detached existence apart from that of the human beings who conduct them. Newspapers are as a rule owned either by one man or a few men, sometimes with long family traditions; or by a public company with perhaps many investors. They are business enterprises, conducted with marked efficiency, gathering and selling news and advertisements, and seasoning the whole with topical comment and criticism. All this is quite proper, even though it has some modern features which are to be regretted.

The editor or controller of the newspaper has a perfect right to criticize, to praise, or to blame, according to the personal opinion of his proprietor, or the joint opinion of his directors or shareholders. He has a right of free thought and free speech with which we will interfere at our own peril. But his right of free thought and free speech is one which he shares with Mr Brown the butcher, and Mr Robinson the bricklayer. He can have no privilege beyond Brown and Robinson; he is equally subject to the laws of defamation. Every good newspaper will admit that you do not purchase any special privilege to defame when you acquire enough money to purchase or found a news-paper; nor do you, in my opinion, purchase a privilege to criti-cize beyond that enjoyed by other citizens. You merely secure a wider audience and, properly considered, shoulder greater responsibilities. For, if Brown libels me, little harm may be done; it all depends on Brown's weight and influence. But if the *Daily Thunderer*, with half a million readers, libels me, irreparable harm is done to me, because people impute to the *Thunderer* a sort of unearthly wisdom and uncommon know-ledge which induces some of them to say, "It must be true. I read it in the paper." Or, more fatuously still, "I don't know, of course, old man, but where there's smoke, there's fire."

If the Press, then, is to see its function in modern society aright, it will dwell on its responsibilities—as indeed I know its best men do—as well as upon its rights, valuable and essential though those rights undoubtedly are.

What are these responsibilities?

Last week I spoke with repugnance of the ever-present political temptation, particularly when the lash of the critic is still smarting, to suppress or issue orders to the newspapers. There is at least an equal temptation on the part of the newspapers to claim the right to suppress the politician, to ignore him if his views are unsatisfactory: to leave him out, not because he says nothing worth saying, but because his views, however admirably expressed, do not suit the paper's policy, or because he himself is out of favour with the newspaper's editor or reporter.

In a word, it is the duty of any newspaper which claims the right of free criticism to publish enough of both sides to make its own views and criticisms intelligible and fair. It is a commonplace of the law of libel that comment must be not only fair, but made on facts. This point is vital to the survival of the Press as a free institution. That this is not always recognized will be clear when I tell you, for example, that for months after my resignation from the Prime Ministership, one newspaper, evidently carrying its hostility beyond defeat, never mentioned my name except in connexion with some entirely false report of my alleged political activities. There was no question of unfortunate error; nor had I become, so far as I know, suddenly and completely mentally defective. The campaign was deliberate and sustained.

Now, that is a mere personal example to illustrate something quite important. The damage done to me is of minor significance. What is really significant is that such a newspaper, following such a practice, is threatened far more by its own inherent misconception of its function than by the activities of its enemies. I say that as one who has never suppressed criticism, even when it was unfair and falsely founded, and who believes that the function of the critic, truly seen, is vital to the establishing of the truth.

There is another tendency among some newspapers to depart

from the old and good journalistic tradition. That tradition was to report fairly and without comment; and, separately, to criticize strongly and, if necessary, bitterly. The public mind was informed by the reporter and persuaded by the leader-writer. But there is to-day a perceptible tendency to mingle report with comment so that you do not know whether you are reading what Brown said or what young Smith, the reporter, thinks of what Brown said.

Reporting of this kind is not reporting at all. It is misleading; it can confer no privilege and excite no respect. That last observation is important. A critic, to carry weight, must be respected. For a man to be respected he must respect others. A free Press must not set itself up to be the master of the people, for in a democratic community the people should prefer the masters they have themselves chosen to those who are merely self-appointed. In other words, a free Press must not seek to maintain its freedom at the expense of popular freedom and popular self-government.

In dealing with men and affairs, the newspaper which claims free speech and opinion as of the very stuff of our liberty—as indeed they are—will no more be restrained merely by the laws of defamation than honest men are merely by the policeman; it will be restrained by that sense of responsibility which should always attach to great power. For the Press has great power, and inevitably so. In a democratic world, great power destroys itself only when it seeks to become tyranny.

And so, let us have a free Press, and let us have free readers whose letters will be published, even though hostile. Let us have honest and fearless criticism of politician by Press and of Press by politician, and let each be heard. Above all, let us get back to "the facts, the whole of the facts, and nothing but the facts" as the true basis of intelligent freedom.

"And ye shall know the truth, and the truth shall make you free." If our diet is to become one of half-truths and prejudice and unfounded comment, either in Parliament or the Press, we shall become slaves.

In time of war these questions, far from disappearing, become particularly acute. The power of censorship offers great temptation to political administrators. The eagerness of millions of people for the latest news, and perhaps excitement, and the natural tendency to look for scapegoats after every defeat offer temptations to the Press. It is unfortunate that both Parliament and Press cannot regard themselves as engaged in a vital joint enterprise in which each must be fearless but restrained; in which each is looked to for good judgment; in which each should look to discharge its own function without seeking to control or discredit the other. In this way authority and freedom would show that they could march side by side to a battle where both must win if either is to survive.

26 June, 1942.

IV

THE FOUR FREEDOMS

Freedom of Worship

President Roosevelt's second freedom is freedom of worship. What does it mean? Do we really understand it? Do we really believe in it?

I remember having a curious conversation once at my back door with an earnest partisan who demanded to know of me—this was when I was Attorney-General of Victoria—why the Government had not prohibited a Eucharistic procession. On my mildly asking why, he opened up on me. "My ancestors," he said, "fought for religious freedom and not to have a lot of people conducting a procession that's an affront to every Protestant."

Now, though a Protestant myself, this took me aback, and when I recovered I pointed out to him—for I gathered that he was a Scotsman—that the religious freedom for which the Scottish Covenanters fought was freedom for all, Catholic or Protestant, Jew or Gentile, and that to deny it was to go back to the dark ages of man. Religious persecution was the denial of freedom. Freedom of worship is the victorious enemy of persecution.

And so I revert to the theme of my broadcast on the first freedom—that freedom, if it is to mean anything, must mean freedom for my neighbour as well as for myself. There is nothing defiant or sectional about a demand for genuine freedom of worship, which is freedom for all.

And what does freedom for all mean? It means, among other things, that we must be free to worship or not to worship. There have been honest and indeed noble men in this world who have never been able to find a God. Are we to deny them their place? There are many men who, profoundly and instinctively religious by nature, have never been able to accept what we call "revealed religion" or the doctrine of any church. There are many millions who find a guide and comfort in life through the doctrine and authority of the church of Rome. There are millions of others who reject that doctrine and authority and, as Anglicans, Presbyterians, Methodists, or otherwise, worship God in their own way. And so one might go on.

We are a diversity of creatures, with a diversity of minds and emotions and imaginations and faiths. When we claim freedom of worship we claim room and respect for all.

Sectarian strife is the enemy of freedom of worship, not its friend. It is the denial of Christianity, not its proof. It is indeed a poor religion which consists merely of opposing somebody else's faith, which produces not faith itself nor understanding nor tolerance nor generosity, but malice and hatred and all uncharitableness.

One of the most upright men and choicest spirits to serve the people in Parliament in my time was the late Thomas Rainsford Bavin, formerly Premier of New South Wales. Himself a Protestant, he spoke as Premier, in 1928, at St Mary's Cathedral, Sydney, during a Eucharistic congress. The small-minded—those to whom freedom of worship means "freedom for my kind of worship, but not yours"—complained.

But what did Bavin say? I quote his noble words:

This cathedral embodies and represents for us those spiritual instincts, that insistent craving for something beyond and above merely material ends which, though often covered up by the dust

C

and ashes of our everyday life, is after all the strongest force in human life—the fountain light of all our day, the master light of all our seeing.

Those instincts express themselves in many forms and in various creeds. They sometimes have led to strife and discord. This should not be so. They should, and I hope will, remind us that the things which unite us as human beings are deeper and more lasting than the things that divide us as members of different creeds. They should be a source of harmony and unity, not of discord and strife; of tolerance and generosity, not of intolerance and bigotry. For, after all, what are they but the gold chains by which the whole round earth is bound in every way about the feet of God?

The Apostle Paul had something like this in mind when he wrote his famous words: "And now abideth faith, hope, charity, these three; but the greatest of these is charity."

We saw on a previous occasion how the Nazi tyranny has struck at freedom of thought and speech; we know how it has also struck at freedom of worship. Not only is the citizen to be told how he shall think and speak of the affairs of his fellow men, but the secret communings of his spirit are also to be controlled. With all our modern cleverness—with our wireless waves and aeroplanes and almost thinking machines—we are still only on the fringes of the universe of thought. We grope out towards the light, seeing an occasional flash of beauty or of understanding, hearing occasionally the penetrating voice of reason. Civilization is in the heart and mind of man, not in the work of his hands. And in the heart of every man, whatever he may call himself, is that instinct to touch the unknown, to know what comes after, to see the invisible.

There is a great instinct in all of us for immortality. There is a consciousness in most of us that some day all will come to light and we shall be judged.

As we put out upon this vast territory of the soul, is there not room for all of us? Shall we turn aside from the search to wrangle, to attack and to defend, or shall we get wisdom and understanding, and with them tolerance, and a true freedom?

To some good people, I know, tolerance means a weak evasion of the duty to denounce and frustrate evil. But they are wrong. We are bound to be enemies to evil when we see it, but we are not bound to be enemies to our fellowman. Tolerance does not mean laziness. The truly free man is tolerant, not of those corroding and corrupting things that all free men will try to destroy, but of other honest men who, hating the same evil, see a different road by which to come against it.

"In my Father's house there are many mansions." That is no reference to the architecture of a physical heaven. All it means is that there is room for all of us, so that we be honest men. Each of us has his own faith, and no mortal man may compel it or suppress it. That is, I believe, a freedom worth fighting for.

3 July, 1942.

V

THE FOUR FREEDOMS

My subject to-night is the third of President Roosevelt's four freedoms—freedom from want.

Here we have one of the most complex of human problems. As we approach it we find ourselves pressed by two considerations, each of which is powerful, each of which acts in opposition to the other. Perhaps in the result we shall find ourselves using these competing pressures in order to establish a firm structure.

On the one hand we have the fact that the struggle for existence and for progress brings out the best in man, and leads, as history has repeatedly shown, to strength and endurance. On the other hand we have the equally clear fact that a never-ending and never-quite-succeeding struggle on the fringe of reasonable existence is destructive of hope and of humanity, which naturally looks for the time, in Browning's words, "when body gets its sop, and holds its noise, and leaves soul free a little".

Let me put the matter in another way. The arriving at a true answer to any difficult problem requires a just balancing of various factors. If our motto is to be, "Each for himself and the devil take the hindmost", then want will be the portion of the least active or the least fortunate, and our civilization will be disfigured by those extremes of wealth and poverty, of comfort and despondency, which have defaced our history in the past, and which a proper understanding of human dignity will roundly condemn.

But if the motto is to be that each citizen is entitled, whatever his own effort or deserts, to a maintenance which will suffice without labour; in other words, that utter security in the economic sense is our divinely allotted portion; all incentive to effort will vanish and we shall become a race ready for the destroyer.

We would need to be blind not to have noticed already in this war the corroding effect of a generation of Government paternalism, of a political tradition of pandering and promises, of a growing belief that life owes the individual the fullest protection and security while the individual owes life nothing at all. We are threatened by the dry-rot of social and political doctrines which encourage the citizen to lean on the State, which discourage thrift, which despise as reactionary those qualities of self-reliance which pioneered Australia.

For a generation in Australia many of us have not been training for the battle of life, but have been disposed to sit back, to rest on our laurels, to leave the struggle to others—in particular, as we are now grimly reminded, to the Germans and the Japanese.

If then, freedom from want means an absolutely guaranteed material life "come rain, come fine", it should not be welcomed by us, for it would surely mean national inertia and decadence. When the poet said, "for we all know security is mortal's chiefest enemy", his statement, odd as it sounds at first, had truth in it.

Should we then reject Roosevelt's third freedom—freedom from want?

Not at all! We should and we shall struggle for it, but we should seek to understand what it means and what it involves. The President is not so superficial as to think that any freedom once purchased may be enjoyed for ever without labour and without sacrifice. Freedom is not a commodity you buy over a counter. It is a principle of life. It must be strong to resist its enemies. It is a source of power, not something passive or dead. My right to be free imposes on me obligations of the most absolute kind to defend my freedom. And so if I am to have freedom from want I must pay the price of that freedom. I must work and strive. In the sweat of my brow must I earn bread.

Thus it is that freedom from want does not mean paid idleness for all. The country has great and imperative obligations to the weak, the sick, the unfortunate. It must give to them all the sustenance and support it can. We look forward to social and unemployment insurances, to improved health services, to a wiser control of our economy to avert if possible all booms and slumps which tend to convert labour into a commodity, to a better distribution of wealth, to a keener sense of social justice and social responsibility. We not only look forward to these things, we shall demand and obtain them.

To every good citizen the State owes not only a chance in life but a self-respecting life. But this does not obscure the fact that the State cannot and must not put a premium on idleness or incompetence. It must still offer rewards to the enterprising. It must at all times show that security is to be earned, to be merited, and is not to fall, like manna, from heaven.

I know that it is or was fashionable to speak of the new order which is to follow the war as if it will represent a sort of golden age of long life, reduced effort, high incomes and great comfort. It is a pleasing picture, but truth requires us to admit that it is probably false. Long years of the ruin and waste of war must be paid for. We shall work harder than before the war, not less. Most of us shall carry burdens greater than those we were accustomed to bear before the war. Materially we may well—as a nation and as a race—be poorer.

But all this will be more than compensated for by the facts that our sufferings and victory will have preserved our spiritual freedom, that our goods will be more justly shared, and that a better recognition of human values will have quickened our sense of human responsibility.

But let me say this in conclusion, that if to most or many of us the war is just an excuse for getting and spending more money, while the new order of our dreams is just a vista of an easy-going and comfortable majority supplied and fed by a laborious minority, we shall most assuredly lose the war, and the new order will be made in Berlin.

Roosevelt's freedom from want is therefore not a fixed and guaranteed state. It promises the just reward for the good citizen. Properly seen, it is not part of a gospel of ease, but calls us to action.

10 July, 1942.

VI

THE FOUR FREEDOMS

Freedom from Fear

When the President made freedom from fear one of his four freedoms for which the Allies are fighting, he no doubt had in mind freedom from international fear; fear of the aggressor nation; that fear of international crime which cast a shadow over the world for years before the war actually broke out.

How are we to win freedom from this kind of fear?

First, by utterly defeating the Axis Powers. The criminal must be resisted and defeated if honest men are to sleep quietly in their beds. And "utterly defeated" means what it says. No compromise, no partial victory will do. However many years of struggle it may mean for us in our generation, there must be no peace without complete victory. A half-won peace would be no better than an armed neutrality. Fear would continue. The volcano would smoke and rumble and no man would feel safe.

It is perhaps easier to say "no peace without complete victory" than it will be to live up to it. We shall all grow terribly weary, and sometimes sick at heart. We shall from time to time find ourselves looking back to those earlier days of peace which, in retrospect, will look so sunny and carefree. But we shall have to conquer weariness and look and move ever forward. For upon our complete victory the future of our race and of the world will assuredly depend.

It is a hard doctrine but a true one that Germany and Japan, the arch law-breakers, the dark angels of fear, must be made to know the whole anguish of war and learn the salutary lessons of defeat. Too often in modern times has war been to Germany an expedition of power and glory on other people's soil. She must know what it means on her own. She must be made to realize that war does not pay; that crime leads to punishment; that the rights of the world are greater than those of the German Empire.

And so of Japan. She, too, has fought her wars in Manchuria and China and the East Indies, and must learn the grim lesson that war comes home.

Second, when victory has come, how is the peace to be kept? For if it is not kept, fear will revive, and the grievous burden of armaments will once more bear down men's minds. Do not let us try to answer this question dogmatically, because we are as yet a long way from winning the war and nobody can foresee the exact shape or even the vague outline of the post-war problem.

But meanwhile, certain things are worth remembering and thinking about. Why did the League of Nations fail to prevent war? Was it because the United States of America stood aloof? Perhaps that was part of the reason. The league, with the United States in and active, would have been much more like a League of Nations and much less like a partial league of some nations.

But that is not the fundamental reason for the league's failure. I am convinced that it failed because it never succeeded in being more than an alliance for certain purposes between certain nations who retained their full sovereignty, their own policies, their own armies and navies and air forces, and prides, and ambitions.

The idea of a League of Nations was that international law

should prevail among nations just as our domestic laws prevail inside our own boundaries. But men live peaceably, and for the most part law-abidingly, inside their own countries for three main reasons: Each citizen gives up his own absolute individual sovereignty in favour of the greater sovereignty of the State and the greater average security and freedom which will result from such sacrifice. It is only in a state of anarchy that men claim absolute sovereignty for themselves. Next, each citizen gives up the right to defend his own security by armed force and in return gets force used as an instrument of the State. In other words, private bodyguards become public police. And finally, the great majority of citizens inside a country have an instinct to obey the law, and that instinct has, as a rule and with no doubt certain setbacks, grown in strength with time.

Now, this third reason will not for many years apply to nations as it does to men. But can the first two?

Would you, if you were in charge of our affairs at the end of the war, be willing for us to enter a League of Nations which was a sort of super-State and which could give us orders?

Would you be agreeable to complete national disarmament, permitting perhaps a small force to restrain domestic violence, and the putting of all armed forces into the hands of the super-State—the League of Nations? The Royal Navy, the Royal Air Force and so on, would disappear. The League of Nations, on a sort of international federal system, would keep the peace while the constituent nations attended to their civil affairs.

If you tell me that this sounds fanciful, I am bound to agree. The difficulties in the way of it are enormous. Our deep-seated national instincts, traditions, may make it impossible. "What?" we shall say, "A sovereign people abandoning some of their own sovereignty?"

And yet we must think earnestly about it, because the alternative to a real League of Nations with real power—and no League of Nations can have real power if all its members are themselves armed to the teeth—is the old system of military alliances, nations being grouped and balanced according to their understanding of their mutual interests. And while nations A, B and C are allies in one group and nations D, E and F allies in another, we can never be free from international fear. It may be that such a system is the only one which is practicable in this world of men, but if it is there can be no guarantee of peace.

Once more I point out that I am not professing to make answers. I cannot see the future. The world may come out of this struggle so nauseated by the destruction and beastliness of war that the most revolutionary ideas on national status will be accepted with quick relief. But, on the other hand, we may come out with such detestation of everything that Germany has stood for that we shall refuse to admit her to any society of nations, least of all one in which we are a relatively unarmed member.

But the point is that, whatever the answer is to be, we shall make it at the right time and place more intelligently if we face up in our thinking to the basic fact that freedom from international fear will require more than a striking phrase, more even than a passionate longing and belief. It will require some international machinery, the blue-prints of which will demand the best brains of every nation.

But governments may be restrained from war not only by force from without but by pressure from within. As Field Marshal Smuts has said, "The individual is basic to any world order that is worth while." If the individual, as in the past generation, neglects politics—except as a means of obtaining some selfish end—then the people will at times of crisis be dumb and impotent, and despotic rulers will make war.

I cannot elaborate this theme at present, but if you reflect upon it you will see that it adds the third and vital element to our analysis. We have seen two of them: a passionate longing for peace, and an international machinery for peace. The third is the motive power for the machine: that intelligent citizenship among ordinary men and women which rulers will respect and which will be the greatest enemy of war.

17 July, 1942.

VII

THE FOUR FREEDOMS

Freedom from Fear *(Continued)*

LAST week I spoke to you about the fourth of the President's freedoms—freedom from fear—with particular reference to freedom from international fear and the things which seemed to me to be necessary if we were to get rid of it.

To-night I want to say something more about the fourth freedom from a different point of view—the local or domestic point of view as distinct from the international. For we must frankly admit that fear has not only been a large and deadly element in international relations. It has also been a recognized and potent instrument of domestic policy. Indeed, a powerful case might be made out for the view that the emotion of fear is the most significant of all the emotions on the field of politics.

Take the case of Germany. The picture so readily conjured up in our minds about living conditions in Germany is one of the shadow of the Gestapo, the spy, the informer, falling across what might otherwise be happy and united homes. When Hitler set up his dictatorship he saw at once that nothing sustains a dictatorship as does fear.

He began a reign which was in every essential particular a reign of terror. Every man knew that though he might be a Nazi in high standing to-day, he might be the victim of a purge to-morrow. And so fear stalked through the land and produced its own iron discipline. Men's minds were beaten upon by highly organized mass demonstrations which left the minority afraid and silent.

And all this was, in its fashion, good psychology on the part of Hitler, for frightened people are much more pliant instruments and much readier receptacles for notions of hatred and revenge than people who move and have their beings in the brave daylight of a free mind.

Now, we recoil from this kind of thing. Indeed, as the war shows, we are prepared to fight against this kind of thing. But when we do, are we fighting an entirely alien enemy? If we look about us, will we be quite satisfied that fear is not an instrument of policy even in a democracy?

Let us reason together quite plainly on this matter because, even if we can never hope at all times and under all circum-stances to be entirely courageous, we can at least hope to be completely honest. If honest, must we not admit that fear colours our political and social life profoundly?

Suppose we are a group of politicians compiling a policy for a popular election. Shall we simply say, "These things are right and good for Australia, therefore we shall advocate them", or shall we, if we are really shrewd men—in the popular sense of the word "shrewd"—ask ourselves what we can promise people in exchange for their votes, or wonder hopefully whether on some issue we can frighten the people into voting for us? Every student of political history knows that there have been political elections in Australia won by an appeal to greed and others won by an appeal to fear. And the fact that they were won shows that the politicians did not misjudge the people. You, the people of Australia, have encouraged these practices. Woe betide the member of Parliament who takes a strong line which is not at first blush the line that his electors would have taken!

Indeed, in recent years a great many people calling themselves democrats have discovered and practised the art of what
is called "pressure politics", the "pressure" taking the form of
hundreds, and in some cases that I can remember thousands,
of stereotyped letters signed and sent to members of Parliament,
on some particular topic, by their constituents, the usual ending
being that "if you do not act in accordance with this view I
will do all I can to have you defeated at the next election".

This kind of pressure, much attempted a few years ago, for
example, by the Douglas Credit people, really represents an
endeavour to exploit the instinct of fear. The hope is that the
member of Parliament will be sufficiently spineless to abandon
his own reasoned convictions for fear of losing his seat in
Parliament.

We may go farther in this examination. It is notorious that
many electors believe that the function of their member of
Parliament is to ascertain, if he can, what a majority of his
electors desire, and then plump for it in Parliament. A more
stupid and humiliating conception of the function of a member
of Parliament can hardly be imagined. If you want mere
phonograph records or sounding boards in Parliament, then
phonograph records or sounding boards you shall get—and
statesmanship will die; and democracy will die with it!

The true function of a member of Parliament is to serve his
electors not only with his vote but with his intelligence. If
some problem arises in Parliament about which he has knowledge and to which he has devoted his best thought, how absurd
it would be—indeed how dangerous it would be—if he should
allow his considered conclusion to be upset by a temporary
clamour by thousands of people, most of whom in the nature
of things could not have his sources of information, and have
probably in any event not thought the problem out at all.

Nothing can be worse for democracy than to adopt the practice of permitting knowledge to be overthrown by ignorance. If I have honestly and thoughtfully arrived at a certain conclusion on a public question and my electors disagree with me, my first duty is to endeavour to persuade them that my view is right. If I fail in this, my second duty will be to accept the electoral consequences and not to run away from them. Fear can never be a proper or useful ingredient in those mutual relations of respect and goodwill which ought to exist between the elector and the elected.

And so, as we think about it we shall find more and more how disfiguring a thing fear is in our own political and social life.

"Men fear the unknown as children fear the dark." It is that kind of fear which too often restrains experiment and keeps us from innovations which might benefit us enormously. It is the fear of knowledge which prevents so many of us from really using our minds, and which makes so many of us ready slaves to cheap and silly slogans and catch-cries. It is the fear of life and its problems which makes so many of us yearn for nothing so much as some safe billet from which risk and its twin brother enterprise are alike abolished.

In time of war it is the absence of fear in individuals and groups which gives dignity and strength to the nation's bearing in the midst of difficulties. It is the presence of fear and the yielding to it which produces hysteria and greed and burden-dodging.

Indeed, when you come to think of it you will see that the belief apparently entertained in some quarters that the people must be kept gloomy if they are to see their duty aright, is in reality a belief that fear is the best emotion for the production of patriotic effort. Nothing could be further from the truth.

Patriotism is the product of courage, not of defeatism. Confidence is the product of a brave optimism; to dismiss it as complacency is to misconceive its nature and gravely to misunderstand its supreme value in a time of trial.

If there was one thing outstanding to the eye when I was in England last year, at a time when the country was being battered every night, it was that there were no signs of fear or of gloom.

It is of course true that light minds flutter easily from one extreme to the other. But balanced minds—sensible minds—will not run readily to extremes. They will see all the difficulties and admit all the dangers; but they will remain cheerful, because they will know that the greatest enemy is neither defeat nor victory, death nor life, but fear.

If freedom from fear is really to be one of the great freedoms enjoyed by mankind, we shall need to prosecute to victory not only our war against Germany and Japan, but a constant war against ourselves.

24 July, 1942.

D

VIII

EMPIRE CONTROL OF AN EMPIRE WAR*

A GREAT debate has been taking place this week in the House of Commons on various aspects of the war, and in particular on the extent to which it is possible to set up representative machinery for joint control.

You will have noticed that in the course of a notable speech, full of characteristic vigour and a refusal to yield to either fear or clamour, Mr Churchill indicated that he was prepared to give to Australia and New Zealand and to any other dominion desiring it, a limited form of representation in the British War Cabinet, the representative having the right to be heard but not the right to join in the making of decisions. In other words, the dominion representative will listen, discuss, and report back to his own Government. Such a scheme has its merits—great me.its—but it stops short of the creation of an Empire War Cabinet. It equally stops short of full participation by, for example, Australia in the British War Cabinet.

Unfortunately, a good deal of the discussion of the last few days has been clouded by misunderstanding of Australia's point of view. To listen to some people you would think that Australia —as yet untouched by any enemy shot or bomb—was suffering from a wave of fear and was sending out a sort of S O S to the world. To listen to some others you would think that Australia,

---

* Events have moved a good deal since this broadcast was delivered but it is included because it may still have some significance.

whose war effort, notable as it has been, stops far short, man for man, of that of the United Kingdom, was full of resentment against the United Kingdom for not having done for us in the past few years things that we were apparently unwilling to do for ourselves. To listen to others again, you would think that the supreme proof of good Australianism is to conduct all your discussions with Great Britain not only publicly but with galleries full of applauding onlookers.

Quite frankly, I denounce all these views as not only thoroughly un-Australian, but as inimical to the best interests of Australia and of the whole Allied cause in this war. Australians are none the less good Australians because they are unhesitatingly British, and there is no reason to doubt that they will meet whatever attack comes to them with the same courage as that displayed by the many millions of people in Great Britain who have known bombing and attack as almost their daily and nightly portion for a long period of time, during which many of us in Australia have lived happily and peacefully in the sun, and have been able to go regularly to the races and the football.

The real problem which has been under consideration this week should therefore be looked at without any of these absurd accompaniments of exaggeration and excitement which have disfigured some of the speeches of some of the partisans.

I believe that the logically perfect thing in this war would be an Empire Executive sitting in London, and full Empire participation in a Pacific Executive sitting in Washington. I say this because I believe that the voice of Australia is a voice entitled to consideration and respect, and because I am a great believer in personal contact and personal discussion. Discussions "inside the family" should not be conducted for the benefit of the neighbours. They should occur in a family conclave, face to face.

I notice with regret that there is a tendency in the last few weeks for ill-informed persons, either in print or over the air, to suggest that my own Government simply said "yes" to whatever the British Government might have put forward. This is utter nonsense, as the world will learn if and when the communications between Governments can be published. But I confess that when I had occasion to put the strongest views direct to Mr Chamberlain and subsequently to Mr Churchill on various matters affecting Australia I did not feel called upon to rush out and announce either that I was doing it or what I was saying. As the Prime Minister of this country, I should have resented the Prime Minister of Great Britain publicly announcing what he was privately cabling to me, and I did not see why the rule should not operate both ways.

Incidentally, of late there have been constant references to what is understood to be an entirely new system by which the Prime Minister of Australia communicates direct with the Prime Minister of Great Britain and the President of the United States.

Now, the constitutional history of our own country is, even under the present urgent circumstances, of great interest to us, and its contemporary facts might as well be accurately stated.

It is no new thing for the Prime Minister of Australia to communicate direct with the Prime Minister of Great Britain. To my own knowledge Mr Lyons did it many times when he was Prime Minister. Equally, I did it many times myself, both with Mr Chamberlain and Mr Churchill, by direct Prime Minister to Prime Minister cables, without the intervention of the Dominions Office, without any red tape or circumlocution. (I should tell you at once that Mr Curtin himself has not in any way claimed that any such communications are novel, but some of his more ardent followers have apparently imagined that they are.) Again, a direct communication between the Prime Minister of Australia and the President of the United States is not novel. For all I know, my predecessor engaged in it. I certainly did on at least one notable occasion in 1940, when France was on the point of collapse.

If any Australian imagines that any Prime Minister of this country would allow circumstances of precedent or red tape to stand in the way of the most direct statements to other people by him, that person is a stranger to the whole modern tradition of Australian Government.

Now, you will be able to make up your own minds as to what you think of this latest move towards giving Australia a representative voice in Empire councils. I may perhaps best help you by sketching very briefly the existing machinery, and I do this because it is far from being well known.

How does the Government of the United Kingdom, engaged in some international discussion, obtain the views of Australia? How does Australia obtain the views of the Government of the United Kingdom?

In various ways. Each day—I am speaking now particularly of the period of the war—the Secretary of State for the Dominions interviews the High Commissioners for the various dominions. He informs them of the discussions that have taken place by the War Cabinet and of the despatches received and sent by the Government. He invites their views. They give them, and he gives his. This is a most useful proceeding, and would be much more useful if the Dominions Secretary were a member of the War Cabinet, which by some curiosity of illogicality, he is not.

Each day the Dominions Office sends circular cables to all the dominions, giving current official news, and almost every day special cables are sent to special dominions about problems which particularly concern those dominions.

While all this is going on in London, each dominion has at its capital a High Commissioner from the United Kingdom. At Canberra we have Sir Ronald Cross, a former British minister of great distinction and ability, and he receives from his Government confidential cables, the substance of which he discusses with the Government of this country.

Periodically, we have the best of all interchanges of ideas when some Prime Minister or minister goes from Australia to Great Britain and meets British ministers on common ground and discusses with them quite frankly problems of common interest.

Now, if you have done me the honour of listening so far, you will at once realize that all this machinery, excellent as it is, is limited by its own nature.

Take the cables. The cable is one of the marvels of modern science and, given the necessary time and space, you can say a great deal in a cable. But the one thing you cannot adequately do by cable is to conduct an argument. The whole thing lacks flexibility. When you receive the other man's cable, instead of seeing him and noting the modulations of his voice, and gather-ing, as you do, the whole atmosphere of the discussion, you simply have a cold-blooded collection of words put in front of you. With the best will in the world you find yourself saying, "Now, what does he mean by that?" You look at some particular sentence and you say, "Well, that might mean so-and-so, and therefore perhaps I should be guarded in my complete accept-ance of it."

These things are the inevitable result of mechanical means of communication.

I tell you quite frankly that when I look back and remember how my distinguished predecessor, Mr Lyons, was abused in Australia because he sent some sort of ministerial delegation to Great Britain practically every year, I almost weep, because if I am certain of one thing, it is this—that these repeated, regular, personal contacts have been the best possible thing for Australia and the best possible thing for the British Empire. If Mr Lyons had taken a foolish, parochial view of this problem, the viewpoint of our country would be much less understood at Whitehall than it is at this moment.

But it has been said in London that while Australia would like this kind of personal Cabinet representation, Canada and South Africa are indifferent to it. Well, it is not for Australia to sit in judgment upon the views of either Canada or South Africa. Each of these great dominions has its own problems and its own point of view. Each of them is to be respected and understood by us. But when all the discussion is over we shall go back to the proposition that, whatever they may want—and that is for them to say—we have most urgently desired an effective voice, at the time when decisions are being made, in the place where those decisions will be taken.

This is not to say that we distrust Great Britain. The expression of my views is, above all, not to be taken as lending any countenance whatever to the miserable grumbling which goes on in certain quarters about the British and what the British are doing in this war. Quite bluntly, when we do as much in this war as the people of Great Britain, we shall have some occasion to grumble—if indeed we feel like it under those circumstances.

I am, like most of you, enthusiastically for the British character of this great Commonwealth of ours. But the truth is that this British character will be best maintained by giving all the adult members of the family an effective voice in the family policy. There is nothing anti-family in that; on the contrary, it is the best way to wage a family war against the marauding outsider.

30 January, 1942.

IX

WHAT THE BRITISH ARE DOING IN THIS WAR*

It would be useless to pretend that Australia is not in more acute danger to-day than she has ever been before. It is equally clear that, having regard to the rapid Japanese progress in the Far East and her great present superiority in the air and on the water, our own unaided defences are not all that we would desire.

In brief, we have reached a point where we must call upon ourselves for the last ounce of man power and material production, and when we are entitled to look also to Great Britain and to the United States of America for the greatest and quickest assistance within their power.

To-night, I want to try to clear up any misconceptions that may arise from some of the circumstances attending our appeal to Great Britain.

The fact that we make such an appeal from Australia is quite sufficient to persuade some people that we are, by implication, criticizing the British for not having given us more help before. It is true that a small handful of people, some of them unfortunately very vocal, would like us to believe that Great Britain has let us down. It is equally true, as I am firmly persuaded, that the vast bulk—the overwhelming bulk—of Australians are utterly and soundly British, and that nothing is farther from

---

* Some of the statements in this broadcast would be modified in the light of recent more happy events, but I have included it as a record of how things looked in February, 1942.

their thoughts than to appear to be reproaching the Government or people of Great Britain at a crucial time like this.

But perhaps there may be a want of knowledge of what Great Britain is doing and an easy temptation to think that somebody else's interests have been preferred to our own. It is in an endeavour to correct this that I am going to say something to you about what the British have been doing in this war.

When I say it, please don't imagine that I am forgetting what Australians have been doing in this war. I am familiar with Australia's splendid war effort from the ground up, and nothing that I say to-night is to detract from the pride and gratitude which we all feel at the courage and self-sacrifice and enterprise of so many thousands of our own people.

But what of the British? It is not my object to make a rhetorical speech about their efforts. All I want to do is to state, almost curtly and in the baldest fashion, some of the things that we ought to remember when we approach them at this time. Great Britain had the courage to go to war and risk everything for a just cause at a time when she was still grievously ill-prepared, when she knew that her enemy was magnificently prepared, and when she knew that that enemy was within an hour's flight of her coasts.

The war opened in almost leisurely fashion, but before the middle of 1940 France had been invaded, and had utterly collapsed; so had half a dozen other countries, and every European port from Bordeaux to Bergen was in German hands. Italy rushed to the kill. The British Empire found itself practically alone in a struggle which, on the fall of France, had assumed a character never contemplated by the most gloomy.

At that dreadful hour—which those of us who were then charged with responsibility for government in this country are not likely to forget—the courage of Great Britain and the flaming spirit of her leader, Winston Churchill, were the defenders of the world and of its future. There was no hint of collapse. There was merely a renewed spirit of dedication.

Had Germany at that time thrown her aircraft and her troops across the Channel, who can say what losses might not have been suffered by the defenders—defenders most of whose modern mechanical equipment had been cast away at Dunkirk?

Before the end of 1940 the air invasion of Great Britain had begun. For eighteen months the men, women and children of that country have taken a battering unparalleled in human history. To their eternal honour they "have not winced or cried aloud".

But let us go farther. What have the armed forces of Great Britain been doing, and where have they been doing it?

Take the navy. It has for over two years sustained the Battle of the Atlantic under terrible difficulties, for every European port was a sally-port against it. Its customary bases in the south of Ireland were gone, and it had to meet a new and most efficient combined form of attack by aircraft and submarine and raiders in constant wireless communication. Its losses have been grievous.

It has largely fed and clothed and armed the people of Great Britain and has kept the supply ships moving day and night. It has controlled great areas of the Mediterranean under the most frightful difficulties. It has convoyed troops—hundreds of thousands of them, including many thousands of our own Australians —and has performed this vital work, I believe, without one casualty. Vastly reduced in relative power since the last war, it has been compelled to scatter its ships over the seven seas— wanted here, wanted there, always on duty—any one ship weeks or months at sea, its crews tired but of an indomitable spirit.

That is the kind of thing that the British navy has been doing at the cost of British lives—many thousands of them—and at the cost of the heavily burdened British taxpayer.

In the air the Royal Air Force, against prodigious odds, has not only saved Great Britain and thereby altered the fate of the British Empire in this war, but in a score of places has gone into action every day.

Many thousands of the flower of the young men of Great Britain have been swept out of existence in the skies.

True, in various theatres of war our armies have been short of air support, but can we honestly say that anybody can be blamed for this except ourselves who, in all our various portions of the British world, laid out our funds in procuring the comforts of life at a time when Germany was forgoing comfort and building up the greatest military power that the world has seen?

I repeat what I have said to you before—that no nation, even as great a nation as our own, can give Germany four or five years' start, and Japan more years' start, and then hope to deal with them both, wherever they may be, effectively in a couple of years.

Then take the British army. It has soldiers in the United Kingdom; some people think too many. But nobody who has been there recently will think them too many, with an enemy only a few miles away and a German army which to-day, after the Polish and French and Balkan and Russian campaigns, contains millions of men who are veterans of modern war.

The British soldiers are not only in the United Kingdom. They are in Gibraltar, Malta, Aden, Egypt, Libya, Palestine, Syria, Iraq, Iran, India, Burma, Singapore. This is an enormous dispersion for troops of so small a country, and it would not have been possible but for the fact that, before the war began the British people had introduced conscription at a time when public opinion in Australia was still, be it remembered, clinging to the notion even of a voluntary militia.

And what of Britain's economic effort? We are to-day acutely conscious of our own, and it is a great one. But the people of Great Britain have had imposed upon them enormous levies by the highest taxation known by any country in the world's history.

Their foreign investments, which made the small islands of Great Britain a rich country and enabled forty million people to do the work of twice their number, have been disposed of for supplies in the United States, and have actually gone by operation of war in other countries.

The people of Great Britain have had their whole lives changed. They have been rationed for food and clothing. They have been living lean. Yet there has been no moan—no gloomy pondering upon a poorer future—but only a high-spirited resolve to hold the fort.

It is not possible in a few minutes to do more than give this bare outline, but if you can listen to it and think about it without profound emotion, then I confess I cannot.

When Australia asks Britain for help to-day she does not ask it of a country which has failed in its duty; she asks it of a country which has done and will do more than might have been expected of any race of men.

It is true that we are being grievously battered in the Far East, and that we shall be battered more before the tide turns. But we must remember that the grim tragedy of Pearl Harbour and the bitter stroke of ill-fortune in the Gulf of Siam, when our two battleships were sunk, altered within a few days of Japan's entry into this war the whole balance of Pacific sea power; and we must also remember that, so to speak, the whole foundation upon which Pacific strategy was based was blown away.

Such disasters cannot be repaired in a few days or a few weeks. It is not easy to assemble quickly from various parts of the world great battle fleets, with aircraft carriers.

Meanwhile, command of the sea has given to the Japanese a fluidity of movement, a capacity for bringing aircraft carriers to the attack, which have been the outstanding reasons for their spectacular successes.

That Great Britain and the United States will bring into this part of the world all the forces which can be mustered I do not doubt. That they may be able to do it promptly I most sincerely pray. But we add best to our own stature, not by contemplating the alleged shortcomings of others but by determining that whatever the British people have done anywhere in the world we can and shall do in Australia. We are a fighting people, and we derive from one.

Whatever comes or goes before the final victory, real Australians will do no dishonour to the blood that is in them and to the example that has been set to them.

6 February, 1942.

X

HATRED AS AN INSTRUMENT OF WAR POLICY

DURING the last week or two a considerable argument has been proceeding about the anti-Japanese publicity campaign officially sponsored over the air and by posters and newspaper advertisements.

I cannot say that I have myself heard or seen a great deal of the propaganda in question, but what I have seen provokes me to make some observations on a matter which, unless quietly considered, may probably lead to misunderstanding and accusations and counter-accusations of an unfortunate kind. It is not a party political problem, for there must be differences of opinion about it on both sides.

The last advertisement I saw, after setting out various arguments, ended by announcing, apropos of the Japanese, that "We always did despise them anyhow."

Now, if I may take that last observation first, it does seem to me to be fantastically foolish and dangerous. It is, in my opinion, poor policy to try to persuade people to despise the Japanese.

So far in this war they have shown us points in most departments of fighting. Their courage is admitted; their skill is much greater than we thought; their resource and ingenuity and capacity for devising novel means of warfare have been at times staggering.

To despise such people is absurd. Such an attitude is merely of a piece with the constant underestimation of our enemies which has been one of our great handicaps in this war. We cannot begin too quickly to develop a great respect for the Japanese as a fighting organism. When we attach a proper value to him in this sense, we shall begin to realize with fullness that we are not dealing with a contemptible enemy whom a second-rate effort will serve to overthrow, but with a tremendously powerful enemy whom we will have to go at full stretch to defeat.

But this is only one aspect of the problem. The real thing that troubles me about this campaign is that it appears to proceed from a belief, no doubt quite honestly held, that the cultivation of the spirit of hatred among our own people is a proper instrument of war policy.

No one wants to be academic or unearthly or super-human on such a matter. We all fall far short of the perfect Christian ideal, and we all—and very naturally at a time like this—have our moments of burning hatred. But the real question is whether we should glorify such a natural human reaction into something which ought to be cultivated and made a sort of chronic state of mind.

I think it was Napoleon who was credited with saying that "hatred is the mark of a small man". And if that epigram referred to continuous and settled hatred, not of the evil in human beings but of human beings themselves, then it was unquestionably true.

In a great war like this, bitter moments are the portion of many thousands of people, and one must respect that bitterness and its cause. But if we are to view war problems from a national point of view and—what is even better—from a world point of view, then we must inevitably conclude that if this war with all its tragedy breeds into us a deep-seated and enduring spirit of hatred, then the peace when it comes will be merely the prelude to disaster and not an end of it.

It is conceded the world over that the Australian soldier is a good fighter. But I have never heard it suggested that he was a good or persistent hater. He has very frequently respected his enemy though he has fought him, and fought to kill.

Do we want to change him, or are these campaigns directed to the civilian? Is it thought that Australian civilians are so lacking in the true spirit of citizenship that they need to be filled artificially with a spirit of hatred before they will do their duty to themselves and to those who are fighting for them?

I remember one night in England last year sitting at dinner with Mr Churchill. The topic of conversation was something akin to the one I am discussing with you. The Prime Mininster, with one of those flashing turns of speech which characterize him, suddenly drew out of the past an observation of his own:

"In war, fury; in defeat, defiance; in victory, magnanimity; and in peace, goodwill."

Don't you think that is a fine doctrine? And note the language. He didn't say, "In war, cold and calculated and cultivated hatred"; he said, "in war, fury". There is nothing artificial about fury, and least of all about the honest fury of an outraged citizen who is determined to defend himself and his home and his beliefs from barbarian attack.

It is an offence to an honest citizen to imagine that the cold, evil and repulsive spirit of racial hatred must be substituted for honest and brave indignation if his greatest effort is to be obtained.

Of course, we live in a world of men and not of saints, and

E

we must not be highfalutin or priggish. But it is not high-falutin to have a noble and decent cause in war. It is the very moral height of our great argument which alone can reconcile the mother to the death of her son in battle. This war is no sordid conflict of racial animosities. If it were, it could never end in your lifetime or mine.

When generals and statesmen sit around the conference table at the end of this war they may make treaties, but treaties cannot alter the spirit of man. Peace must not only close the door on war; it must open the door to better things. It is not by treaty that we shall pass out of this hideous valley of death into the higher lands of peace and goodwill. Peace may be all sorts of things—a real end of war, a mere exhaustion, an armed interlude before the next struggle. But it will only be by a profound stirring in the hearts of men that we shall reach goodwill.

In short, when this war is over we all hope to live in a better world in which both Germans and Japanese, violently purged of their lust for material power, will be able to live and move in amity with ourselves and in that friendly intercourse which is a more powerful instrument of peace than any artificial plan ever devised.

This does not mean that we are to be soft or hesitant or anything other than determined and ruthless in our search for victory. It does not mean that in some dreamy or philosophic fashion we are to forget that the salvation of mankind requires that this generation of ours should be ready to go through hell to defeat its devils. But it does mean that we should refuse to take the honest and natural and passing passions of the human heart and degrade them into sinister and bitter policy. We shall, in other words, do well if we leave the dignity and essential nobility of our cause unstained and get on urgently with the business of so working, so fighting and so sacrificing ourselves that that cause emerges triumphant and the healing benefits of its success become available as a blessing not merely for us but for all mankind.

10 April, 1942.

XI

SCRAP IRON FOR JAPAN

To be a Prime Minister and then an ex-Prime Minister is to find yourself charged with most of the crimes in the calendar. In my own case I have discovered that one of the most current accusations made about my administration is that we sent iron to Japan and that the Japanese are now using it in the form of munitions against us. Indeed, only this morning a printed circular has reached me which demands legality for the Communist Party of Australia and which goes on to describe this party as —and I now quote the exact words—"declared illegal by the Menzies (pig-iron-for-Japan) Government in June 1940."

Now, I can assure you that I am not a bit concerned to defend myself against the ridiculous charges which are always made against public men, but as some decent people may be worried over this particular question, I shall just say a little to you about it.

My term of office was from April 1939 to August 1941. So far from the Menzies Government being a "pig-iron-for-Japan Government" the records show that, during my term of office, no pig iron was exported from Australia to Japan, nor was any iron ore. In the whole of the two years the exports of steel to Japan from Australia did not reach fifty tons.

It is true that over the same period there was an export of one hundred and seven thousand tons of scrap iron to Japan from Australia, while in half that period, namely the year 1939 alone, the United States of America exported to Japan two million tons of scrap iron and the like material. Make a note of that—the U.S.A. in one year exported twenty times as much as we did in two years.

During my term of office Australia exported to Japan one hundred and ten million pounds' weight of wool, valued at £8,000,000, and £1,700,000 worth of wheat. About these last two items I have heard no complaint, though it is obvious that the maintenance of any army depends upon food and clothing just as much as it does upon guns and ammunition.

The other material fact you should have in mind is this, that while we did export to Japan a relatively small quantity of scrap iron which was not needed in Australia, we at the same time were importing from Japan substantial numbers of lathes, grinding machines and other tools of high quality, badly needed for our own munitions programme.

It is a pretty unfair sort of judgment which directs its attention solely to what Japan got from us while completely ignoring what we got from Japan.

I am still quite satisfied that the policy of the Australian Government in relation to trade with Japan was right, and has been in effect very much to our benefit. In the first place, if Australia had prohibited the export to Japan of materials—whether scrap iron, wool or wheat—capable of military use, we might very well have provoked this war with Japan at a much earlier date than December 1941.

Weighing up the whole of our present position, can anybody in his right senses imagine that this could have been to our advantage? Do not forget that the fact that Japan did not enter this war against us until she felt herself ready to make the United States her first enemy is of great importance to us, and will unquestionably lead to her ultimate defeat. Was Australia,

the smallest country concerned, to be the one country to hit
Japan on the nose?

Heroics about this kind of thing are all very well after the
event, but sober students of international relations who had
any knowledge of the extent of our warlike preparations were
and are quite satisfied that victory for the allied nations depends
upon well-co-ordinated and synchronized effort, and that, before
the war with Japan began, the best prospect of influencing Japan
lay in combined action on the part of the democratic countries,
not by sporadic and foolhardy action on the part of the smallest
of them.

What some people do not appear to appreciate is that in this
modern world with its rapid communications, Governments
which have interests in common do not act, so to speak, in
watertight compartments. They keep in touch with one another.
They prefer united action to disunited action, and it is just as
well for our prospects in this war that they do.

Second—and I am saying these things to-night in an attempt
to settle an argument, not to stir one up—why make this
purely unreal distinction between iron and wool? Iron and
steel have their civil as well as their military uses. Wool has
its civil as well as its military use. It is clear enough to-day
that many thousands of bales of Australian wool have probably
gone into Japanese uniforms, and a soldier cannot fight without
a uniform. The clothing of an army is a major problem.

You may say that we have helped to clothe the Japanese troops
fighting against us. But if you are going to be quite frank with
yourselves, go out into the kitchen and see what Japanese crockery you have in the house. If you have some, please remember
that Japanese crockery sold abroad created for Japan some of
the very credits which have enabled her to equip herself for
war.

The world's trade, if it is to be in reality fluid and far-reaching, cannot be confined to individual localities. Nations cannot live to themselves, and in the long run the traffic between two nations must flow in both directions if it is to be of real value to either.

In result, therefore, I urge you to pay no attention to these whisperings, however widespread they may be. If Australia sinned in exporting scrap iron to Japan she was, all things considered, the smallest sinner among the allied nations. If she sinned in exporting wool to Japan, she was one of the greatest sinners among the allied nations.

But in reality there is no question of having sinned at all. The whole economy of this country has rested upon our great exports, and upon the willingness of foreign countries to buy them.

In the last two and a half years we have had much reason to be thankful that because of these things our financial stability has been high, and our resources so great as to enable us to put forward a war effort—particularly on the productive side—that nobody would have imagined possible a few years ago.

3 April, 1942.

XII

THE CENSORSHIP

To-night I want to speak to you about the subject of censorship. It may be a disappointing thing to say so early, but I do not propose to make an attack on the censorship, or even upon the censor, whose displeasure I have so far never incurred. What I really want to do is to discuss with you one or two aspects of wartime censorship which seem to me to require plain thinking.

The essence of the principle of wartime censorship can perhaps be expressed in one sentence—that censorship imposes silence, and silence is one of the important weapons of war.

Censorship has two main subject matters: opinion and news.

The censorship of opinion raises difficult problems. The task of the authorities is to permit criticism and to prevent subversion; to avoid political censorship, but to maintain a complete repression of anything that threatens the national security.

Time will not permit an analysis of this interesting and important problem, but you will all have your own ideas as to how it should be solved.

The other aspect of censorship, that of news of and arising out of the war, is the one about which I would like briefly to talk to you.

In the handling of news—of statements of fact, or alleged fact—is the censor being too severe or too lenient? Are we being told too much, or too little? Is the enemy reading our newspapers and listening to our broadcasts with profit to himself, or not?

My own answer to these questions is that though, from time to time, there are mournful complaints about an excessive censorship of news, I believe that there is too little. There is too much talk of a kind useful to the foe and, if I may say so quite bluntly, there is too much talk anyhow.

Of course, you have me on the hip at once. I can hear some of you muttering to an unresponsive wireless set that such a sentiment comes badly from an almost notorious speech-maker; but I shall stick to my guns. Sinner as I am, I shall still condemn the sin. There is too much talk.

At the moment the most successful Allied leader is Stalin, and he must be one of the most silent men on earth.

We British once used to regard ourselves as "strong, silent men"—not voluble and excitable, as other nations were. Alas, "how are the mighty fallen"! Every day and every night we vocally exhort, explain, denounce, comment, prophesy; political statements flood the already saturated air; boys of tender years whose knowledge of strategy is non-existent expound, in paragraph or column, the deficiencies of generals; after every defeat we have a noisy and ill-informed post mortem for the benefit of a delighted enemy; we talk of morale so much that we are in danger of losing it.

The truth is that most of us have no adequate conception of the use that may be made by our opponents of quite simple-looking disclosures of fact.

Many a time I have heard people say, apropos of some item of news—perhaps the presence of some ship in an Australian harbour, freely discussed down the street but banned from the Press, "Oh, what nonsense to conceal it! If we know it, the enemy must know it. His system of espionage, of intelligence,

is perfect." But when you consider how little *we* know of what
our enemy is doing—of his equipment, his aeroplanes, his ships,
his personnel—and how inaccurate what little we thought we
knew has turned out to be in most cases, why should we assume
that he is in any better plight than we are? And why should
we take any shadow of a risk of telling him something that he
does not know? One indiscreet statement in a newspaper column
or in a broadcast may to-morrow or next week sink a troop-
ship, or submit an air base to attack, or cut off and destroy a
division.

Frankly, listeners, I have been horrified—as I am sure you
have been—at some matters which find their way into print
or come across the air in relation to movements of troops, of
ships and of aircraft.

When the defence of Johore was about to begin, one heard
over the air and read in the public Press of certain changes in
the disposition of the Australian forces. That must have saved
the Japanese a great deal of difficult and dangerous reconnais-
sance. When the *Prince of Wales* and the *Repulse* arrived at
Singapore, their arrival was shouted from the house tops. Whenever it appears that we are deficient of either men or equipment
in some part of the world, we take the world into our confidence
and advertise the fact to all comers. Such things are dangerous.
We all like news, but news is much less important than victory.

I do not know whether it has always been so in our history,
but it is hard to believe that any war has ever been conducted
with such an accompaniment of publicity—individual publicity
with all its false values, the splashing of the lightest words of
amateurs across the world's newspapers.

Apart altogether from my deep-seated belief that whatever
in this strange, mad world of ours is best advertised, is probably
the worst in fact, what I want to emphasize is that no considera-

tion of publicity should ever be permitted to impose three ha'p'orth of risk upon any man fighting for his country.

And we cannot leave all this business of censorship to my unhappy friend the censor. There is such a thing as self-censorship, self-restraint. Some of the stuff we have served up to us from day to day might well be made the subject of a self-denying ordinance.

Most people are not fools, and they are not easily satisfied by a common form of news-announcing couched in such cheery and exaggerated terms as to make it seem that the war had been an unbroken series of victories for us. We have all noticed that whenever the enemy retreats he is, so we are told, "broken"; his retreat is a "rout". During our recent push in Libya, and at a time when any rational onlooker must have admired the extraordinary skill and tenacity and resourcefulness of the German general, Rommel, the announcer over the air kept telling us that Rommel was still "on the run".

But whenever *we* retreat, we are doing it "according to plan". We are doing it to "prepared positions". A cynic would think that all our retreats were planned in advance.

Such false pictures do nothing but harm. We shall win this war not by bluffing ourselves about the facts but by facing them, without necessarily advertising them.

It is foolish to go on telling ourselves or being told that if enemy aeroplanes are destroyed on the ground it shows unreadiness or even fear on the part of the enemy, while when our aeroplanes are destroyed on the ground the incident represents merely misfortune of the blackest dye.

The whole danger of induced self-deception on the news of the war is that we either become completely sceptical of the truth of everything we are told or, accepting it, we sink more deeply into a condition of stupid underestimation of the

enemy—an underestimation that has done us incredible harm
in the past and that is quite capable of destroying us unless we
take steps to destroy *it*.

It is time that we "cut the cackle", to use the homely phrase,
and set out with a clear recognition of the facts in our minds,
and with one object—to become as good at and as well-prepared
for war as out opponents. We shall not fight any the worse if
we concentrate on the business of fighting and of producing, and
save our breaths until we really have something to say.

We shall not remain indefinitely inferior to the Japanese in
sea power or in air power when once we have frankly admitted
that we are inferior and that we must be prepared to submit
to all the discipline that he imposes upon himself—and more
—if we are to catch him up.

A completely candid self-examination would, I believe, show
us that a good deal of our trouble arises from the fact that our
belief in our innate and almost godlike superiority to "the
foreigner" is dying hard, but is not yet dead.

We have fed ourselves on miserable and false clichés. "One
volunteer," we have said, "is as good as two pressed men."
What nonsense! For the two pressed men may be of the highest
courage and skill, and superbly equipped. "We lose battles but
we win wars." What pitiful wishful thinking that is! "Our
beautiful battleships will never be outmoded by the bomber."
And then the enemy comes along with dive-bombers and torpedo-
carrying aircraft and sinks two of these monsters in a matter
almost of minutes.

And while we are slowly—but surely, I hope—ridding ourselves of these self-deceiving doctrines, some of the foreigners
to whom we were so superior are setting us the most noble
example of resourcefulness, of self-forgetfulness, of stark and

realistic courage. Look at the Russians on the German frontier! Look at the Dutch in and around Java!

These reflections may seem to you to have little or nothing to do with censorship. As I see them, they have a great deal, for the function of censorship, as I began by saying, is to impose silence.

The function of self-censorship is to create silent places in our own minds and our own hearts: a modest silence when we think how far we have fallen short in this struggle; an admiring silence when we think how much some others have done; a determined silence when we contemplate the task in front of us, and the labours which we must endure before it is completed.

6 March, 1942.

XIII

THE NEW MINISTER TO WASHINGTON

THE Government has recently appointed Sir Owen Dixon to succeed Mr Casey as Australian Minister to the United States of America.

The term "minister" is occasionally confusing to people because we normally use it in its political sense, whereas in the case of these oversea appointments, both the title and the post are diplomatic.

I wonder if we are always clear in our minds as to the function of a diplomat, and in particular of an Australian minister accredited to the U.S.A. A cynic said many years ago that a diplomat was a man who was sent abroad to lie for his country, and though we have no doubt got over that idea there must still be many people who believe that the chief function of such a man is to eat and drink and make after-dinner speeches. There can be no greater mistake. In modern times, and particularly at a time like this, the function of a diplomatic representative is of the highest gravity and complexity.

Just let me occupy a few minutes in describing, for example, the nature of the work which has to be done at Washington by the Australian minister to that capital.

First, he is the direct representative of His Majesty's Australian Government, and as such he has a heavy individual responsibility for the dignity and reputation of his own country. This is not to be underestimated. Representatives of other countries are much in the public eye, and their fellow countrymen are liable to be judged favourably or badly according to the standard they exhibit.

Second, the minister is the channel of communication through which important and intricate matters are discussed with the President of the United States, with his most important ministers, and so on. This does not mean that our minister is a sort of postman who merely conveys, for example, to Mr Cordell Hull, what the Australian Government is thinking, and then sends back to the Australian Government what Mr Cordell Hull's answer may be. Important discussions are not conducted in that fashion. They contain an exchange of ideas, argument, explanation, suggestion, and they cannot bear fruit unless the men taking part in them are of such a calibre that they meet each other on proper terms and with a proper mental equipment. It follows from this that an Australian Minister to Washington requires much more than a capacity for easy good-fellowship. He requires education, knowledge, skill, flexibility of mind, a constructive capacity, and marked judgment.

Third, he must keep our Government in Australia informed as to the opinion and policy in the United States. He must have and transmit, not vague notions but positive ideas. This requires that he should have a penetrating eye and a clear understanding.

Fourth, he will have a golden opportunity to impress the significance and quality of Australia upon the American mind—that is, the American public mind. By his various public speeches and broadcasts he is enabled to direct the thoughts of perhaps millions of American citizens towards Australia and its problems, not as things possessing merely geographical flavour, but as real matters of urgent international importance and of great significance in the winning of the war.

And finally, he has many economic and financial matters to handle, of the details of which we can know but little. Take, for example, the vast network of complicated problems which surround the assistance that the United States of America is giving to the Allied nations under the Lend-lease Act.

On the face of it, that Act authorized the raising and spending of great sums in America for the provision of materials of war to the Allies, not in exchange for cash or for some set future liability, but on a basis which still remains flexible, if not actually vague. In the atmosphere of generous impulse in which we now live, the implications of lend-lease assistance to the Allies may attract but little attention. But surely it is quite clear that when the war has been won the Allied nations, including our own, will need to have far-reaching mutual adjustments of an economic kind if the friendly and intimate association of the war is to be a powerful and good thing in time of peace.

During this war we have all been, willynilly, forced into the most acute development of self-sufficiency or, as it has been called, "economic nationalism". There will need to be a lot of reconstruction of our ideas some day—not, of course, with the idea of hindering our own development, to which we properly attach immense importance, but with a view to using the resources, for example, of the British Empire and of the United States of America to the fullest mutual advantage.

Even while the war is on, great wisdom is needed in the handling of these matters, and the part to be played by the Australian Minister in Washington must be of major importance.

Now, having as I hope indicated to you the first-rate importance of the work Sir Owen Dixon goes to take up, I should like to add a few words about Sir Owen himself. I am perhaps not unqualified to do this for, when I first went to the Bar, I was a pupil in his chambers—his first pupil, I am happy to recall—and for many years I have known him intimately, both professionally and personally. I speak of him, not as one sitting in judgment but as a profound admirer.

He is a scholar in the truest sense, in a period in which pure scholarship has been somewhat jostled on one side by what we are pleased to call "more practical matters". He is a lawyer of the first water, challenging comparison with any other lawyer in the English-speaking world. He is a man of shining integrity and high outlook, with a Spartan simplicity of personal habits which recalls the old tag about plain living and high thinking. He has an immense capacity for work. Frequently when I was his pupil and we had worked in his chambers until midnight, I was staggered to learn next day how much he had apparently accomplished in the way of really hard legal work between then and the following morning.

When the war broke out, an interim judgment upon him might have been that in the academic and legal worlds he had achieved pre-eminence, but that he was relatively unacquainted with affairs. But that interim judgment must now be overhauled. In the last two or three years, as chairman of the Central Wool Committee and as chairman of the Shipping Board, he has, on the evidence of all interests—and, if you like, on my own as Prime Minister for a considerable portion of that time—displayed administrative gifts of a high order; all of which goes to show that though a man may not, as in the case of Sir Owen Dixon himself, have had any political experience, there is no branch of knowledge which need remain closed to a man of ability, application, and wide comprehension of mind.

As I have said, I was his pupil when I first became a barrister.

F

I need only add that I have been learning from him in a variety
of fields ever since.

He does us much honour by representing us abroad. Washington will come to know him and to value him as a most
distinguished representative of the best Australian culture and
civilization.

15 May, 1942.

XIV

OUR AMERICAN ALLIES

It is very natural that, when we find ourselves in alliance with a great nation like the United States of America, we should get to know something about its people.

When you consider the modern speed of travel and communications, the easy flow of literature, the almost ubiquitous character of the moving picture, it is astonishing how little we know accurately of people who live only a few thousand miles away from us.

We know very little about the Americans, and, if I may aspire to be Irish for a moment, a great deal of what we do know about them is not knowledge at all. Only a few Australians have ever been in America, and consequently the impressions of most of us are derived from materials which are much more frequently picturesque rather than correct.

I wonder if it would be useful for me to take a few minutes in just stating, and if possible correcting, a few of the most current misapprehensions?

The first is that the United States is an Anglo-Saxon country, full of our cousins, and that because of this intimate family relationship Americans must either automatically be with us in any world dispute or seem a little queer and uncousinly. This is a fundamental error. It has been calculated that if the *May-flower* held all the ancestors who reputedly crossed to America in it, it must have been considerably bigger than the *Queen Mary* or the *Queen Elizabeth.*

True, up to the closing quarter of the nineteenth century it might accurately have been said that the United States was substantially and ultimately of British stock. But the subsequent vast movements of migration altered all that. Many millions of United States citizens have their family origin in Germany, Italy, Russia, Poland, the Scandinavian countries. We cannot automatically think of the United States any longer as an Anglo-Saxon community, but we can and do think of it with great pride and satisfaction as a community in which the language, the literature, the institutions and the ideals of the British people have taken root and flowered.

The second matter is to be found in the old allegation that Americans are intensely commercial, and that their actions are dominated by the "almighty dollar". When I hear people in Australia saying that, I am always tempted to say, "He that is without sin among you, let him cast the first stone." Can we honestly say that we are superior to the pursuit of the dollar? We in Australia have our absurd aristocracies of money. We do not yet adequately understand that making money, though some people have elevated it to a science, is as a rule the lowest of all the arts.

I wonder if we realize that, allowing for the difference of population, proportionately more people read seriously, think seriously and go out for higher education in the United States than in Australia? The ordinary honest citizen with just one wife and a family for whom he has ambitions and for whom he is prepared to make sacrifices, provides no copy for the moving picture scenario-writer or for the sensational newspaper and so, when he is an American, we do not hear much about him in Australia. But I assure you there are many millions of him.

The whole atmosphere of the United States is most stimulating to anybody who really believes that there is more in life than dollars and that the development of the mind is one of the real foundations of progress.

Again, what of the American Press? Almost every time I see a film I am informed that American newspapermen wear villainous hats, pulled down in front, and keep them on while they chew cigars, invade private houses, clutch a telephone with each hand and put innocent citizens through the third degree. It is very picturesque, and perhaps it is true of crime reporters—with whom my acquaintance is, oddly enough, limited—but in point of fact the newspapermen by whom I have been cross-examined in the United States are conspicuously the best-informed, the quickest and the shrewdest that I have encouncred anywhere in the world.

Then there is the American judiciary. If one were to go by our current sources of information, one would have the impression that American courts deal exclusively with divorce and that their proceedings are conducted with a strange and hilarious mixture of sentiment, comedy and melodrama. But in fact the best judges and other lawyers in the United States are great lawyers by any measurement—just in the same way as American surgery occupies a high place in the medical world, and American architecture at its best is "a thing of beauty and a joy for ever", and none the less a joy because its plumbing has been attended to by real experts!

The last example I shall deal with is the current belief that Americans are not as realistic as we are: that they have a vein of idealism and even of sentimentality not found in the hard-headed Australian. Well, I would be the last to condemn idealism, because it is the ultimate motive force in human development. But when it comes to realism, it is necessary to point out that, a year before this war began for the United States, it had introduced conscription, though it was a neutral country and was and is a democratic country. When we remember how many entirely sentimental objections we have to practical and frequently necessary policies, it is not for us to be the critics.

Let me turn away from this brief sketch of some of our misapprehensions to say something positive about the Americans.

One has always had a vague feeling that in the long run the greatness of a country can be tested by its production of great men. If we apply this test to the United States, it is to-day surviving it magnificently. Let us take public men alone. I say "alone" because it is a fallacy to think that greatness is to be found only among those who control great political affairs.

But let us take public men. Among Americans to-day, we shall find Franklin Delano Roosevelt, Cordell Hull, John Gilbert Winant.

President Roosevelt has entered upon his third term of office. He is the first President in the history of the United States to have a third term. When his people voted it to him they broke a tradition that went back to Washington. No common man can be accorded such a distinction. Indeed, Roosevelt is a most uncommon man. He is singularly endowed with the graces of life. He is a man of great personal charm and magnetism. He has that quiet and smiling humour which we so readily understand. His selective command of language is remarkable. He is perhaps the most effective living politician: his knowledgeable finger is always on the pulse of public opinion.

Each of these things is a useful attribute for a great man to have, but not one of them of itself will make a man great.

Roosevelt's greatness proceeds from a combination of two things: First, his indomitable courage. No man, stricken down by infantile paralysis in his adult years, who literally rises from his bed to become three times the President of the United States is to be denied that superb attribute. No man whose political programme puts him at odds with almost everybody in his own circle, and who pushes on with it, can be denied admiration. And second, his far-reaching and sensitive understanding of the real problems of common humanity.

In 1935 when I was passing through the United States, every newspaper was attacking Roosevelt; all the people of a conservative or comfortable turn of mind were belabouring him; he appeared to have no "big" friends. Yet he has passed from triumph to triumph.

Contemporary valuations are all too frequently astray, because superficial and flashy qualities weigh too heavily in the scales of contemporary judgment. But, allowing for all this, we may surely name Franklin Delano Roosevelt among the greatest of the Presidents of the United States.

Then there is Cordell Hull. If he ever reads these words of mine he will forgive me for describing him as looking, at first sight, like an extremely prim, solemn and tucked-up New Englander. But on contact that impression weakens. He has a flash in his eye, an edge on his drawling tongue, a cutting quality in his mind, which indicate life and vigour. His personal prestige in the United States is enormous. He speaks with the authority of character. He is trusted. He is no parochialist to be concerned only with his own country. For years he has struggled with the vexed problem of world trade. Isolationism could not be part of his creed, because he not only sees men as social beings, but nations as social units in a world society.

In a decade so characterized all over the world by the crudest policies of national self-sufficiency, the existence at the State Department in Washington of a liberal and humanist like Cordell Hull has been of the first importance.

And finally there is John Gilbert Winant, the American

Ambassador to London. I am most honoured to number him among my friends. Tall, rangy, with a raven lock of hair falling over his forehead, with jutting eyebrows, deep-set eyes and a long, strong jaw, he looks something like a clean-shaven Abraham Lincoln. He is a rich man who has devoted his life to the service of the poor. He is a shy man—shy sometimes almost to the point of speechlessness—but he has forced himself to take an active part in public affairs in the United States, at the International Labour Office, and now at the American Embassy in Great Britain.

In speech he is not what we call a typical American at all. He does not hurl his words at you. On the contrary, they appear to float reluctantly from some remote corner of his mouth. You must listen closely to catch them all. But words are chiefly of value for what they convey; and in Winant's case they convey the product of hard and clear thinking by a mind of rare reach and flexibility.

He is an ex-soldier with a passion for peace and great dreams of social and industrial improvement, but at the same time with a rock-like determination to stamp out the Nazi spirit—a determination which was not only obvious but comforting long before America had actually entered the struggle.

Here are three men whom we can venture to describe as great men. The country which is able to place them in three key positions of public service at a time of supreme crisis is a fortunate country and makes a great contribution to the world.

Now, I am—like you—dyed-in-the-wool British, and have a firm belief that the courage, humour, tenacity and resourcefulness of our own race never shone more brightly than now. The fortunes and aspirations of Australia are linked with those of Great Britain "for better or for worse; for richer or for poorer;

till death do us part". But it is a great thing for us to have such allies as these Americans.

We are together now for the urgent saving of the safety of the world. When that task is over, I hope that we shall remain together for the keeping of that safety for ever and ever.

23 January, 1942.

XV

LEND-LEASE

ONE of the many troubles, I was going to say of democracy, but perhaps I should say of ourselves as a people, is that we do not think enough and that we take too many astonishing things for granted. Too many of us are like the old man in the story who said, "Sometimes I sits and thinks, and sometimes I just sits."

To-night I want to talk to you about one of the most astonishing things that has occurred in this war—a thing which was so staggering when it was initiated that it riveted the attention of the entire world, but which has now become a mere phrase in most people's mouths.

In March of 1941, with America still neutral, with Russia neutral, and with the British nations battling along against great odds, the American Congress, at the instigation of the President, passed an act which was called "an Act to promote the defence of the United States", but which has become much better known as the "Lend-lease Act".

It was a short statute. It defined defence articles in very wide terms, then proceeded to confer upon the President power, from time to time—whenever he deems it in the interest of national defence—to authorize the manufacture or procurement of any defence article (I now quote the exact words) "for the Government of any country whose defence the President deems vital to the defence of the United States".

After providing for the selling, exchanging, leasing or lending of any such defence articles, the Act makes this pregnant and historic provision:

the terms and conditions upon which any such foreign Government receives any aid shall be those which the President deems satisfactory, and the benefit to the United States may be payment or re-payment in kind or property or in other direct or indirect benefit which the President deems satisfactory.

Under this Act and supplementary appropriations the most enormous effort is being put forward in the United States, while in countries like Australia benefits are being received by way of material aid which could probably never have been paid for in dollars under an ordinary commercial system.

When I tell you that the amount of lend-lease aid that may be provided under the various Acts amounted, in March last, to nearly twenty thousand million dollars—to say nothing of many thousands of millions of pounds' worth of goods that can be transferred to Allied countries—you will see that this great scheme represents the most novel and spectacular move ever made by a great nation still occupying, as America did at the time of its passage, a technically neutral position.

You will recall that in the last war vast borrowing and lending transactions took place between the Allies. Great Britain provided enormous sums for Russia, for France and for Italy, and most of those loans were not repaid. The United States of America lent large sums to Great Britain, the interest on which was met for a number of years until, in the depression, its further payment in full became impracticable. This failure of Great Britain to meet her war debt to the United States occasioned a great deal of criticism and discussion, and in some quarters tended to impair the relations between the British and the American peoples. For many years economists and statesmen of all the formerly belligerent countries were exercised about international financial and commercial relations, one of their great problems being international war debts.

As the present war developed and American opinion, under the wise leadership of President Roosevelt, became more and more clearly pro-Ally the President saw with statesmanlike insight that the time was going to come when British dollar resources for the purchase of much needed supply would become exhausted, and that if thereafter British loans had to be sought in the United States a problem full of unhappy potentialities would once more develop. He decided to avoid this, and the result of his decision was the Lend-lease Act.

Now, what does the Lend-lease Act really mean?

Its immediate effect is that British and Allied countries, including our own, make requests to the appropriate authorities in the United States for the supply of appropriate materials, and when these requests have been dealt with and approved, and the necessary orders have been issued to American manufacturers or producers, and the necessary goods have been supplied, those goods are delivered to the requesting country without either immediate payment or specific debt.

The Agreement which the United States made with Great Britain in February of this year is perhaps typical of those which will be entered into generally. Its outstanding provisions are:

First, that the Government of the United Kingdom will return to the United States of America at the end of the war such defence articles transferred under the Act as shall not have been destroyed, lost or consumed, and as shall be determined by the President to be of use to the United States. Second, that in the final determination of the benefits to be provided to the United States by the United Kingdom in return for lend-lease aid, the terms and conditions shall be such as not to burden commerce between the two countries but to promote mutually advantageous economic relations between us and the betterment of world-wide economic relations. To that end they shall include provision for agreed action by the United States and the United Kingdom, open to participation by all other countries of like mind, directed to the expansion of appropriate international and domestic measures of production, employment and the exchange and consumption of goods which are the material foundations of the liberty and welfare of all peoples; to the elimination of all forms of discriminatory treatment in international commerce, and to the reduction of tariffs and other trade barriers; and, in general, to the attainment of all the economic objectives set forth in the Joint Declaration made on August 12, 1941, by the President of the United States of America and the Prime Minister of the United Kingdom.

In other words, payment as I understand it, is not visualized as a sort of pecuniary rental or purchase price for the goods, but is to be found in post-war economic arrangements which will be for the mutual benefit of all parties and of the world, and will tend to minimize the acute economic nationalism which preceded the war.

You will at once appreciate the significance of these steps, begun, I remind you, at a time when America was not actually participating in the war, but undoubtedly produced by a profound feeling in the United States that the battle for Britain was in reality the battle for the civilized world.

We in Australia should not take all these things for granted. We should prepare our minds to understand that while the full development of the industrial resources of Australia is something dear to our hearts and, as we think, good for everybody, we cannot expect when the war is over to live in a little watertight compartment of our own.

A world war makes us a world nation; not a parochial community, but a world community. Nothing so contributes to peace among men as the maintenance of ordinary, decent commercial relations, and these relations can be restored only by the most liberal statesmanship when the war is over. That the problems will be difficult nobody can doubt. Making trade a two-way traffic is always more popular with those who buy than with those who sell. It is to be hoped, however, that the people of all nations, and particularly those who come within the lend-lease network, will realize that peace will bring its problems, much more complicated in many ways than the problems of war, and that those problems will admit of solution not by people who have abandoned reason and clear thinking, but by those who really believe that a permanent new order for the world will demand hard work, tolerance, a wide vision and mutual understanding.

Looked at in this way, this great lend-lease movement, though for the moment it appears to solve great problems, will produce even greater ones, which it will be one of the principal tasks of post-war statesmanship to overcome.

29 May, 1942.

XVI

WOMEN IN WAR

THERE is no more popular fashion than that of calling ourselves realists. But what is "realism"? Surely it is a state of mind in which the thinker has put on one side all sentiment or prejudice or self-delusion. In other words, realism involves facing the facts, whatever they may be, and acting in accordance with them.

On no question is a realistic approach so necessary but so rare as it is on the question of the war employment of women. To-night I want to take a few moments of your time in clearing up, if I can, your minds and my own on a problem which is of increasing importance and urgency.

We have grown up with what might be called all sorts of taboos and superstitions and conventions on this matter. We say, perhaps a little artificially, that women should not do this or that kind of work, and that if circumstances do require that they should work, the task should have a quality of gentility.

Now, what is the truth about the kind of work that women can do—and particularly about the kind of work that women can do in war? I should like to answer that question by reference to my own experience of observing war work in Great Britain last year.

Many hundreds of thousands of women were actively engaged in the war effort—not only in nursing and hospital services, but in scores of other ways. The Auxiliary Territorials were doing clerical work, were driving cars, were carrying on administrative activities. At operational headquarters of branches of the air force I saw hundreds of young women in uniform doing, with speed and accuracy, work of the greatest importance. At the fire stations of London, scattered right through the blitz area, there were hundreds of women—young and not so young— dressed in the blue overalls of the auxiliary fire service; not merely standing around and looking picturesque, but working hard and fast, reporting fires, telephoning, doing a mass of clerical work which before the war was done by men.

And it did not end there. When the bombs came down and the fires started there were young women of the auxiliary fire service driving cars, driving other vehicles, operating courageously in the fire-lit target areas, coping with incendiary bombs, sweating and grimy, but playing a part worthy of any brave man.

Just before I left England, selected women were being introduced into active army operations, doing particularly some of the precision work involved in the anti-aircraft defences.

In every munitions and aircraft factory that I saw, there were hundreds and sometimes thousands of women employed. Some of them of course were doing fine inspection work where lightness of touch and accuracy of eye produce speed and output. But these were a relatively small proportion. Most of the women at work were dressed in overalls like men, attending to lathes and presses, using riveting machines, wielding hammers, doing in many instances downright hard manual labour.

As I saw them they were cheerful, with good nerves, with the right enthusiastic spirit.

I was told more than once that on a morning after a blitz in some industrial area you could almost bank on one hundred per cent of the women employees being on time for work.

In the country districts the increased production which is

being wrung from the soil of Great Britain is in many instances being wrung from it by the hard physical toil of women of the land army.

On every street the woman bus-conductor is a familiar sight.

So there are hundreds of thousands of women in uniform, in overalls; but there are millions of women who, while they form part of no army and work in no factory, are doing a superb job in an entirely unadvertised and often unnoticed way. To-day's housewife in Great Britain has had the whole order of her life disturbed. She has become a great improviser, a person of almost infinite resourcefulness. If the bombs fall and the electric light system is interrupted or the gas mains are set on fire or the water pipes burst, she must be able at almost a moment's notice to turn her hand to getting, by what means a man can never understand, a hot meal for her family, because the day's work must go on and the day's workers must be fed. After dinner at night, sitting with her family in her suburban street, she may find herself called upon to go out with sand bag and stirrup pump to help to extinguish incendiary bombs in her area.

What a life! And what amazing courage this is that can take daily danger almost as a commonplace!

And, apart altogether from bombs and destruction, this same housewife is the one who has had to adjust the routine of household management to rationing—the rationing of food, the rationing of clothing, the rationing of almost everything that people buy.

One could go on for a long time with a catalogue of this kind of thing. But, in brief, it all represents a formidable breaking down of old barriers and old ideas.

No doubt this great movement of women into the defence of the realm is destroying or impairing some elements of life which we might have liked to keep. But we shall be completely

G

unrealistic if we do not realize that when this war is over there
will no more be a return to the *status quo* for women than
there will be such a return to many of our older notions of life.

Now, what are the paramount questions that we in Australia
must answer in relation to this problem if we are to face frankly
our dangers, and therefore our needs?

The dominant one must be this: Have we ample man power
for all the tasks of this war—including not only the fighting
services, but muntions production, essential civil production both
primary and secondary, and essential civil services? (When I use
the expression "man power", I mean man power and not woman
power.) Plainly, we have *not* ample man power for these needs
in the light of the new and extending and pressing demands
of this war.

Well, then, can we achieve our end by drawing upon woman
power? Plainly, we *can* to a very great extent. There *should*
be no prejudice on this matter. There *must* be no prejudice on
this matter.

Wherever a woman is willing and able to do some job, however "unwomanly" that job might have seemed to the eye of
convention or of custom a few years ago, and her employment
in it will either give us something we lack to-day or release a
man for a job, fighting or otherwise, which only a man can do,
then there should be no barrier against the woman doing it.
On the contrary, there should be active encouragement and
direction. That seems to me to be the essential principle of this
matter.

Somebody may say to me that this lifting of many women
out of ordinary domestic affairs, this taking down of woman
from her "pedestal" is fraught with grave dangers for the future
of the race.

Perhaps it is, and perhaps it isn't. But the gravest danger to the future of our race is that we shall be defeated in this war, and we must be prepared to take much greater risks than the one to which reference has just been made if victory is to be ours.

Really, I do not think we need fear the future on this matter unduly. There is—and every year I live, every new experience I have convinces me of it more and more—there is a courage, energy, skill and resource about women which can serve this land mightily.

And if that is true, will the country not be all the richer because those qualities have been put to the highest patriotic use? In the long run, will our community not be a stronger, better balanced and more intelligent community when the last artificial disabilities imposed upon women by centuries of custom have been removed?

There is no equality so ennobling as an equality in service. There is perhaps nothing we need more as a corrective to the patent ills of democracy than a full brotherhood and sisterhood in action and sacrifice.

When peace comes and we try to resume our normal lives we will, I believe, learn one thing among others as a result of our experiences in this war. And that thing will be that those thousands of women who will, before this trial ends, serve Australia with all the strength of their minds and hearts and hands, will be the better mothers of the new generation because in this one they have been the fighting daughters of their country.

20 February, 1942.

XVII

PAYING FOR THE WAR

As a great war loan is about to be launched by the Government, it seems appropriate that I should this week say something about the importance and significance of war finance, and why, in a phrase, we must spend less if we want to fight more.

We must not regard such questions as being either remote or merely technical. They possess both gravity and urgency. We must, every one of us, back the Government's efforts to see that no civil action, no civil spending, no notions of ordinary comfort or personal advantage, must be allowed to stand in the way of doing all that we physically can to win this war.

The financing of this great struggle is not, as some of us may imagine, a mere matter of collecting cash from those who have it and spending the proceeds of the collection upon paying fighting men and adequately equipping them with arms. Wars are not fought with money, but with men and materials. How do we get men and materials? The answer surely is, by subtracting them or diverting them from the ordinary affairs of life.

If hundreds of thousands of men go into the armed forces they can no longer live their ordinary lives in a civil way. If scores of thousands of men and women go into munitions production they can no longer do their ordinary work in civil production. If hundreds of thousands of tons of materials go into the munitions factories they can no longer go into civil factories. If millions of pounds of purchasing power go into the war effort they can no longer go into civil buying.

In brief, a war effort is a subtraction from normal civil effort. We cannot have it both ways. We cannot have our cake and eat it too. That is why the Government must ask us to go without things we normally buy, if we are to have those military things without which we cannot fight.

Let me put the matter in another way from the point of view of the ordinary citizen. I do not want to appear pedantic on such a question, but I am firmly convinced that the golden rule of citizenship is that each of us should act as he would wish all other citizens to act. That is why individual decisions are of such immense moment. That is why every citizen must test this matter for himself and be earnest to discover his own duty.

John Jones is in steady employment and earns £8 per week. This is more than he was earning before the war. If he spends all his £8 on his current desires at the shops and other people act in the same way, the civil business turnover will increase very much: the big department stores will have record sales, and the demand for civil goods and civil services and civil factory production will not fall, but rise. And, as we have seen, because no man can at the same time be a soldier and a civil worker, and no piece of metal can at the same time be used for a shell case and also for some household article, the civil demand set up by John Jones and all those who think with him will, if it is satisfied, keep some men out of war service and some materials out of war production.

Now, listener, if you happen to be John Jones, drawing your £8 per week, you may want to retort to me, "Nonsense! It's the big man who has the purchasing power. Let him economize! Let him subscribe to the loans!" But you will be wrong. The Government is attending to the so-called "big men": an income tax of fifteen or seventeen shillings in the pound instead of five shillings before the war is a pretty effective economizer. And out of what is left we are still expecting that the big man will be able to put something into war loans.

But the bulk of the purchasing power of Australia is not in the hands of big men. In 1940-41 the individual incomes of Australians totalled £800,000,000. Of this total £560,000,000 represented incomes up to £400 a year. In other words, seventy per cent of the total of individual incomes is earned by people whose individual earnings do not exceed £8 a week. If you think for a moment you will realize that it is in this group that the greatest increase in wartime emoluments has occurred— as a result of overtime, war loadings and much more constant employment. It has been calculated that in the first two years of this war the income of this group increased by a total of £70,000,000.

I mention these facts because I want you, Mr John Jones, to understand your own importance in war finance. If you want Australia to put forward £250,000,000 of war effort this year, your contribution is essential. For the fact is that if you say no, and all others in your position have the same point of view, the war effort will not be achieved.

And what goes for John Jones goes for everybody, big and small. Not one of us can stand out. If we do not buy less and spend less on our own civil requirements, Australian troops will not get their full equipment and we shall fight this war under grave, and perhaps overpowering, handicap. We have never before had a war like this one, and we pray God we shall never have another. This is not a war in which subscription to war loans can be the safe investment of the rich, or the casual handing over of an easily acquired and easily spared surplus. "All-in war" is not a mere pithy phrase. We must not use it as a substitute for clear thought or resolute action; it must be a stark reality. "All" does not mean "some"; above all, it does not mean "a few".

Now, listeners, it is necessary to be quite frank about this problem, and to ask ourselves how we are measuring up to our responsibilities. It is a poor and demeaning pastime to criticize the other fellow when our own conduct falls short of reasonable standards. Great Britain has forty-five million people, and we have seven million. We have for years enjoyed conditions of life unsurpassed anywhere in the world, and materially better, more comfortable, and more conducive to saving than those obtaining in Great Britain. Since the war broke out, the level of taxation in Great Britain has risen to saturation point. I do not think anybody will seriously suggest that British taxes have not "socked" the rich to the limits of endurance.

Salary- and wage-earners in Great Britain, particularly those on the smaller incomes, pay more taxes than in Australia. Yet, since the war broke out, Great Britain had raised, up to the end of October 1941, £1,737,000,000 of war loans and £385,000,000 in national savings certificates. The corresponding figures in Australia, from the outbreak of war up to the end of January 1942 are: War loans, £113,000,000; war savings certificates, £30,000,000.

A short calculation will show that, on a population basis, to compare with the effort in Great Britain, we should have subscribed £260,000,000 in war loans and very nearly £60,000,000 worth of war savings certificates.

Subscriptions to national savings certificates in Great Britain or war savings certificates in Australia are expected to be made by those of limited means, for the limit of individual holdings in Great Britain is £500, and in Australia £250.

These figures and comments constitute a real challenge to us to decide whether we are really pulling our full weight and making our full individual share of sacrifice necessary to sustain a winning war effort.

When I say this I am in no sense intending to use the language of complaint. That there were, until the incursion of Japan into this war, many thousands of people in Australia who regarded the war as distant and perhaps not dangerous, can scarcely be denied. But, while such a point of view exhibited not only a want of knowledge but also an absence of clear thought, it was human enough in all conscience. We never see distant dangers as clearly as we see near ones. Bushfires assume more dreadful proportions the nearer they come to your own house or your own farm. The danger of an invasion of Great Britain is, quite naturally, viewed more philosophically from this distance than the danger of an invasion of Darwin is at this moment.

Having regard to these considerations, it must be said that the Australian public has responded well to the call for funds. But in this year of 1942 it must, if it is to do the job, respond twice as well. No man should run away with the idea that there is much real patriotism involved in taking a few war savings certificates during the year so that he can cash them at Christmas-time in order to buy a new suit of clothes. The Government wants two things, and I hope I have been able to make them both clear to you to-night.

First, it wants the use of your money—every penny of it that you can spare after providing for a modest and decent way of life—and it wants that money not for a month or two, but for years. Second, it does not want your money merely as money. It wants you to hand funds to it for war expenditure so that you will not be spending that money on those competing goods and services which use up man power and materials urgently and grimly needed for war.

I do beg of you that you will not allow yourselves to be side-tracked by any foolish theory that we can go on living and spending as if we were at peace, and that by some mystery of the financial system soldiers can still be raised and paid and equipped and the country fight its way out of its deadly peril.

What I have said to you is not one-sided, or political. In reality, I am merely trying to reinforce, with such authority as you may accord to my knowledge and experience, what the Government of the day is in substance saying to you. On this great matter which touches and concerns the sinews of war, we must all be prepared to back our Government, and by so doing save ourselves.

13 February, 1942.

XVIII

POST-WAR PLANNING

THE practice of calling on those in authority to produce the blue-prints of the new world that is to come after the war is not quite as popular now as it was before Japan came in. We are pretty urgently engaged as a nation in fighting to preserve that portion of the world which we have and in which we live. In consequence, there is a good deal less discussion about the future, and plans for it are for the time being at a discount.

On this problem, as on others, it is possible to run fairly readily to extremes, one man saying, "Leave post-war problems alone until the war has been won", and another saying, "Unless you define to me what sort of new order is to come after the war, I'll have to let you win the war without my help."

As so often happens, both extremes are wrong. If we come out into peace in tolerable shape but with not one idea on post-war policy in our heads, we shall almost certainly enter a period of slump, confusion, bitterness and disillusionment terrible to contemplate. On the other hand, if we, so to speak, down tools in the middle of war to work out what we shall do after the war, we shall lose the war, and the new order will be Germany's and Japan's, not ours.

Surely the real answer is that, without subtracting from the full power of our war effort, and without engaging in full-dress philosophic debates in an atmosphere hostile to their success, we should, as and when opportunity presents, provide facilities for competent and practical study of post-war problems by a few sensible and trained people in appropriate places.

This is not a topic that can be exhaustively discussed or even adequately outlined in a few minutes, and so to-night I shall do no more than illustrate the kind of thing I have in mind. And let me say that it has assumed some clarity in my mind largely as the result of some recent stimulating conversations with Mr C. S. Teece, the commissioner of patents, whose knowledge of industrial patents is far-reaching, and whose enthusiasm is infectious.

The essence of wartime production is the transference of machines and skill and effort from peace products to war products—the beating of ploughshares into swords.

We have seen this in dramatic fashion in Australia.

In Great Britain the Board of Trade has wisely given wide publicity to some of its features. I have before me an advertisement by the board in an English trade journal of May 1941. It reads, under the caption "Emptying Shelves and Filling Shells":

In wartime, production must be for war and not for peace. Here are examples for the changeover from peacetime prodution to wartime necessities:

> Corsets become PARACHUTES AND CHINSTRAPS
> Lace curtains become SAND-FLY NETTING
> Carpets become WEBBING EQUIPMENT
> Toilet preparations become ANTI-GAS OINTMENTS
> Golf balls become GAS MASKS
> Mattresses become LIFE JACKETS
> Saucepans become STEEL HELMETS
> Combs become EYESHIELDS

Now, when peace comes, the process will have to be reversed. We shall have to beat our swords into ploughshares again. Parachutes—to follow the words of this striking advertisement

—will have to become CORSETS; gas masks will have to become GOLF BALLS; steel helmets will have to alter their shape and become SAUCEPANS. But the thing to note is that this reverse process will be by no means automatic. It will require careful planning and prompt action at the right time.

And we must take the matter farther. In Australia, for example, we have not merely changed over existing industrial equipment: we have created a mass of new equipment and undertaken a mass of new manufactures. The anti-aircraft gun, for example, is a marvellous piece of precision engineering, done to a degree of accuracy far beyond the normal by means of machines and instruments of which we knew but little three years ago. That is why it is easy to decide that you will make anti-aircraft guns but difficult to accomplish the long process of assembling your plant from other countries, designing and making what you cannot buy, laboriously tooling up with jigs and gauges and so on for mass or repetitive production. But, thanks to many people, all these things have been done in many factories.

We are turning out hundreds and hundreds of munition items we had never previously attempted; and this means trained operatives, new materials, an immense variety of machine tools, and concentrated experience in their construction—scores of new techniques. What is to become of these things when at long last the war ends, and many hundreds of thousands of men with vital claims upon their country have to be readapted to a happy and busy civil life?

I notice that Mr Berle, an Assistant Secretary of State in the United States of America, recently, in an article on post-war development, urged that every defence industry should have a research staff working on plans for producing out of the resources and experience of that industry peacetime goods, and preparing catalogues of products that will become available when the war ends.

I agree warmly with this suggestion, which can be given a very wide application. Such a scheme would not require great numbers of people, but its significance and value would be enormous.

When, as Prime Minister, I set up the Department of Labour and National Service, provision was made within its structure for research on post-war problems, and some useful work has been done. But on the industrial or manufacturing side the Munitions Department, with its colossal and concentrated experience, may well be a more appropriate place, just as planning on the agricultural and pastoral side is appropriate to the Department of Commerce, and planning on the financial side appropriate to the Department of the Treasury.

The whole essence of this idea is that a little forward-looking and really concrete work by a few people not actually or actively engaged in the immediate business of war production may save us from grave errors and lost opportunities when the war is over.

The view is, I know, held in many quarters that the immediate post-war period can be most effectively helped by large programmes of public expenditure on public works. But this has never seemed to me to be a permanent cure or to provide a really satisfactory repatriation in the true sense of that word. We shall not only have to find occupation for demobilized soldiers. We shall have to find alternative occupation for many scores of thousands of munition workers.

The best way of doing both of these things is to put ourselves in a position where we can use promptly and with a high degree of effectiveness all those things we shall have learnt in war, applying our technical ability and experience for the satisfying of civil needs when the war has been won and those civil needs can once more demand satisfaction.

I end with this warning. The winning of the war is the paramount business; all else is secondary. But though secondary, we shall forget it at our own risk.

17 April, 1942.

XIX

RATIONALIZATION OF INDUSTRY

A PROPER reminder by Mr Fadden this week that while rationalization of civil industry during war was essential, there was and is no popular mandate for socialization, has elicited from the Prime Minister the comment that he sees no justification in time of war for having forty brands of tooth paste. How far this comment is an answer to the criticism you will no doubt decide for yourself. Meanwhile, it might be useful to consider the whole problem of wartime rationalization—quite briefly, of course—in order to see whether there are any principles which ought to govern it.

At a time like this a mere battle of long words will not do very much good to anybody. It will certainly not solve any difficulties. Nor will the business notions of people whose only claim to being unprejudiced is that they know nothing of business aid us very much.

The whole question goes far deeper than words, and not one of us can hope to solve it by rhetoric—a commodity, by the way, as yet unrationalized, although responsible for an almost alarming consumption of man power.

You will of course realize that it is quite impossible to make any sort of adequate or scientific analysis of our subject in the space of a few minutes. But at the same time we may get an approximate picture if I endeavour to state, quite shortly, a few principles to which I believe the great majority of reasonable people will subscribe:

1. No Government in time of war, whatever its political colour, ought to be politically embarrassed simply because it is compelled, for the winning of that war, to do some damaging or unpopular things. Just as we all naturally would like to receive a share of the credit for good things done which are popular, so we ought all to be prepared to accept our share of the responsibility for good things done which are unpopular.

2. On the other hand—and this is my second principle—no Government in time of war can or should escape criticism or, if necessary, attack, if it does damaging things which are in fact unrelated to the successful conduct of the war, or are done only to further some partisan political end such as socialization. The current answer to most criticism—"There is a war on!"—cannot possibly justify a suspension of the sober critical faculty or the supine acceptance of industrial and political ideas which most people have been resisting for a lifetime and which they believe do not represent the objects for which the war is being fought.

3. The rationalization of civil industry, that is, the reorganizing of that industry so as to avoid waste and damage to the war cause, is a process which can and should at this time be legitimately carried on for two main purposes. One is the curtailment of civil expenditure; the other the release of man power, including woman power, for war work.

Civil expenditure must be reduced simply because military expenditure must be increased, and we cannot simultaneously spend our money on both. The most direct means of achieving this reduction is by taxation—and, as I think, though Parliament has not yet agreed, on *all* incomes. Another means is by loans, which take up the savings of the people and, if patriotically understood, encourage them to make further savings. Another means is by rationing goods and rationalizing industry. As we reduce civil demands for goods and services, so we reduce the supply, and workers at the supply end are set free for war work. So also are other workers engaged normally in the distribution of those goods or the organizing of those services.

That is the simple theory of rationalization.

4. If the Department of War Organization of Industry, which was set up in my own time and, in fact, by me, for the very purpose of rationalization, and to which as a department I take no exception whatever, seeks to curtail or alter any industry for purposes other than those already mentioned, it cannot object if people begin to wonder whether some doctrinaire political and social ideas are not being experimented with by means of purely wartime powers which were designed for war purposes, and without a popular mandate at a general election.

Great principles may occasionally be tested by small examples. Let us therefore take the otherwise soothing and refreshing subject of tooth paste. Let us assume that there are forty brands. If there are, it proves that there is a market for forty brands, each of us buying his special choice. Now, along comes the Government, represented by the Department of War Organization of Industry, and says, "In future you shall have the choice of, say, three brands only."

Will the result of such an order be that the public will, in total, spend less money on tooth paste? I think not—and indeed, in a sense, I hope not. I, for one, shall use as much as in the past. So will you. We don't really believe that the price will fall, and so we shall, as a nation, spend as much on tooth paste as before. There is therefore, no curtailment of civil expenditure on this item.

But is there a saving of man power? Well, there may be. I do not know, and we have not been given the facts to enable any of us to know. If the department could tell us that reducing

H

tooth pastes to three would release so many scores or hundreds or thousands of men and women for essential war work, or even as many as the average number on strike during the past three months, there would be a good case to consider. But what are the facts? Unless they are given to us, we have no means of judgment, and those engaged in the tooth paste business will feel all the inconvenience and loss produced by the new rule without the compensation which would arise from knowing the measure of benefit conferred upon the national war effort by their own sacrifice.

All that we can say is that, unless it is clear that there will be a real release of man power, any government should move warily. For, wiping out thirty-seven brands of tooth paste would not merely reduce the variety of flavours and colours we can squeeze on to our toothbrushes: it would wipe out for the war thirty-seven good wills and trade names or marks, laboriously and expensively built up in time of peace. In the case of all goods sold under special trade names the asset of goodwill is of immense importance. It is just as important to its owner as the asset you have in the savings bank or a house or an insurance policy is to you. To destroy it may be necessary in war, just as we should destroy a building impeding the field of fire of a battery of defensive artillery. But, unless it is necessary, it is wanton.

You will see that I offer no opinion on this aspect of the tooth paste case. I use it merely to illustrate and give point to the questions which good wartime administration should constantly put to itself.

Take another example on which some of us may have definite opinions of our own—the rationalization of banking. If the requirements of man power really necessitate the closing of some branch banks in centres where other branch banks can do the business with a reduced total staff, well and good. There is no sanctity about a bank. But when the Minister for War Organization of Industry says, in one breath, "the trading banks such as the Bank of N.S.W., the National, the Commercial and so on, must be curtailed and many of their branches must be closed to release man power" and, in the next breath says, "But this is to have no application to the Commonwealth Bank," he must not be surprised if people conclude either that he thinks that Commonwealth Bank employees have some special defect which disqualifies them for war production, which is absurd, or that the cutting down of the trading banks, which to-day do the overwhelming bulk of the banking business transacted by ordinary citizens, will build up the Commonwealth Bank—which is rank socialization and undisguised party politics.

To sum up: I should think that most people in Australia, whatever the inconvenience to themselves, will face up loyally to a rationalization of industry in the sense and for the purposes I have tried to indicate to-night, because they will feel that the one thing that counts is that we should win the war, and that to win it there must be no waste of man power and no distraction of effort. But I am equally confident that most people will resent any intrusion at this time of purely partisan conceptions which can do nothing except divide us at a time when we shall most readily find our truest strength in real unity.

24 April, 1942.

XX

TAXING THE SHAREHOLDER

One of our greatest temptations in a democracy is to accept a slogan as if it contained "the truth, the whole truth, and nothing but the truth". If some proposal is superficially attractive, we are not very disposed to examine it closely. It is unhappily true that we do not examine and criticize ideas half so strenuously as we examine and criticize men.

The recently announced intention of the Government to limit company profits to four per cent on shareholders' capital is a splendid example of the kind of superficially attractive proposal which, when examined, proves to be utterly and incurably unsound.

It is supported by two very popular notions: First, that in time of war, four per cent is quite enough for any man to earn on his money. Everybody sympathizes with that. Indeed, most men with money would be quite happy to be sure of earning four per cent on it. Second, the vague notion that most companies are rich and that, as they have a sort of separate existence of their own, you can tax them almost to the limit and no great harm will be done to any ordinary man or woman.

You may go beyond these two ideas and tell me that it comes with ill grace from the capitalist who has so large a stake in the country to complain about losing some of his profit in order to support the war.

Having thus looked at some of the arguments which underlie this proposal, let me now turn to what I believe to be the truth on this problem.

I am not a bit concerned to defend the position of the rich. As I have said to you on previous occasions, they can as a rule look after themselves, and their hardships are in any case relative and not absolute. But I *am* concerned, and increasingly concerned, with the ordinary middle range of people in this country—those who are not rich and yet, urged on by a spirit of independence, endeavour in spite of every parliamentary discouragement, to provide for their own future. These people are the salt of the earth, and if the moral future of this country is to be saved it must be saved by them. They are the most precious element in our nation, and I shall hope to fight their battles so long as there is anybody to listen to me.

Let me, in order to test the proposal now under examination, take a typical case of a small shareholder in a company. John Jones has worked hard all his life. He has never enjoyed a large income, but on his salary of a few hundreds a year he and his wife have acquired a home. They have brought up a family. They have undergone real sacrifices in order to give the best possible education to that family. They have been good citizens, and have contributed a family of good citizens to their country. Year after year they have put a little by for their old age, because they look forward to an old age in which they will look the whole world in the face and stand on their own feet. As their small funds have accumulated they have invested them—not speculatively, but in solid and successful Australian undertakings conducted by well-established companies.

In the case of John Jones, he has invested in a leading industrial concern which has been paying a dividend of eight per cent for a number of years and whose shares he has from time to time bought, not at a pound each but at market prices ranging from thirty shillings to two pounds a share. This has meant that the funds John Jones has invested for his and his wife's old age return to him, not eight per cent but perhaps, on the average, five per cent, taking into account the price he has paid for the shares. He has, at the time of his retirement from active work, achieved an income from his shares of £200 a year, on which he proposes to spend the evening of his life.

The Government comes along and, in the sacred name of an attractive slogan, tells his company that its dividend must be reduced to four per cent. John Jones's effective dividend is at once reduced to two and a half per cent, and his income from £200 to £125. He and his wife are at once brought to a point where they are given to understand that they might just as well have saved nothing, and drawn an old age pension from the Government.

This is not an uncommon case. If is becomes common, the results will be disastrous to Australia. If we are to retain our virility, our pioneering spirit, for the labours that lie in front of us, we must put a premium on saving and on independence; we must not penalize them.

Now, if you have accepted the view of the soap-box orator that most shareholders are rich men, you may say to me that my example of John Jones is such an unusual one that no conclusions can be founded upon it. My reply to that is that all the records show that the average shareholding of the individual in a company is a small one.

The whole point of the company system, the joint stock system, was that it gave to small investors an opportunity, in association with hundreds or perhaps thousands of other small investors, to have an interest in a big concern.

The whole development of manufacture and of commerce on the grand scale dates from the introduction of the joint stock system. We have much for which to thank it. It is a most important element in the whole of our modern industrial growth. It provides vast numbers of people with employment. And the more successful the company the more continuous will be the employment that people derive from it.

You cannot build increased and happy populations on a foundation of unsuccessful enterprises.

In brief, a very wealthy individual may build up his own business and carry it on successfully. But the vast majority of successful companies are nothing more or less than aggregations of individuals, ninety-five per cent of whom are not wealthy at all, and none of whom would have the opportunity of investing in business except through purchasing company shares.

In result, therefore, we see that, though a company has an independent and separate existence in point of legal theory, it has in substance no existence apart from its shareholders. Its profits are of no moment except in so far as they pass into the hands of shareholders through dividends.

It is of course true that the capital value of shares might be built up by a company accumulating excessive reserves out of profits. But the taxation authorities have for years known the answer to this. Parliament has taxed company profits and war profits in the hands of vast companies themselves, and they have directed particular attention to special forms of taxation upon undistributed profits.

Beyond the setting aside, therefore, of reasonable reserves to meet future rainy days, companies have no inducement not to distribute a large proportion of their profits to their share-holders. So you will see that the best and fairest way of taxing profits is in the hands of the actual human beings who get them. And when we tax human beings in respect of their income, we try to do so on the basis of their ability to pay.

A shareholder with many thousands of shares and an income of some thousands a year may be properly asked to pay an income tax of fifteen shillings or more in the pound. But would it be fair to ask another shareholder with an income of a few hundreds a year to pay a tax of fifteen shillings in the pound? Of course not. One's sense of justice would be revolted at such an idea.

Yet this proposal to cut down dividends of ten per cent or eight per cent or six per cent to four per cent is in reality nothing more or less than a proposal to inflict the same rate of reduction, which is in substance the same rate of tax, upon all shareholders, whether they have many shares or few and whether their incomes are great or small.

There are other aspects of this problem which are, properly considered, of great importance.

When you limit all companies to a profit of four per cent you are setting out to destroy that search for efficiency which leads to one company making eight per cent while a competitor makes only five per cent; and it is at all times damaging to a country to destroy or discourage initiative and efficiency.

When you take steps to prevent a company from building up effective reserves you are imperilling the future of that company, for difficulties are bound to occur in the future, and the company which has reserves is much more likely to weather them than one that has nothing to fall back upon.

It would, for example, be a foolish thing to prevent these hundreds of war industries which have been built up in Australia from establishing reserves adequate to carry them through the period of readjustment when the war ends. And when I say that, I am not primarily concerned with the company as such or with the shareholders as such, but with the capacity of the company to give employment at a time when there will be scores of thousands of ex-service men wanting employment and wanting re-establishment in civil life.

But the main point that I wanted to make to you to-night is that these proposals, superficially attractive as they are, violate the first principles of financial justice, represent an entirely unfair and unbalanced system of taxation, and amount to yet another attack upon those thrifty and independent people who count for so much in the solidity and progress of our country.

31 July, 1942.

XXI

HAS CAPITALISM FAILED?

A WEEK or two ago a friend of mine, putting to me the argument for some kind of socialism, opened up by saying, "Well, for a start, you will admit that capitalism has failed." My answer, which was regarded as astonishing, was, "On the contrary, I think it has been, all things considered, an extraordinary success."

I want to discuss with you to-night the implication of that answer. Sweeping generalizations seldom constitute good argument, though they have a mouth-filling character, and an air of finality very attractive to most of us: "Christianity has failed"—because we are at war, and brute force seems triumphant. "Education has failed"—because ignorance and prejudice are still more powerful than reason. "Democracy has failed"—because democrats have neglected their political duty for a generation. And so we might go on with our catalogue of resounding failures. How absurd it all is!

Christianity has not failed. We shall really have to try it before we declare it a failure. Education has not failed. It is we who have attached too little value to it. Democracy has not failed. It is a neglected child, but it is far from dead.

Well, what of capitalism? What is it, for a start?

Capitalism, as I understand it, is that system of social arrangement which recognizes and protects private property and encourages and protects private production and business enterprise for profit. It is a system under which, during the last century, we have seen enormous developments in the recognition of human rights, in living standards, in material comfort, in public health. It is also the system during the currency of which we have had slums, unemployment, poverty, war.

It is open therefore to comment both good and bad, though you will agree that it can scarcely be held responsible for this war in which the capitalist democracies and the greatest communist State in the world are engaged in fighting a national-socialist enemy. But we can agree that the products of capitalism have been mixed. Is this a ground for abolition or amendment? And if we abolish capitalism and try socialism or communism or some other scheme almost inevitably designed and controlled by someone who has failed at capitalism, are we really confident that we shall get a system under which we shall have the good things of capitalism but with no slums, no unemployment, no poverty and no war?

To answer these questions requires some steady thinking. My own has led me to two conclusions, each of them strengthened by some fourteen years of experience of public administration and political experiment and growth.

The first of these conclusions is that there can be no real prosperity and happiness for all if we merely redistribute the world's wealth without adding to it. In other words, a static material civilization, with enterprise stifled by an iron-bound equality, with the dead hand of the State in control, will mean stagnation, and stagnation will ultimately mean a poverty which will be none the less real because it is shared by all.

If our material civilization is to produce improved and improving standards it must have a dynamic quality. It must aim constantly at progress. And as there can be no progress without enterprise, the encouragement of enterprise in the most direct human fashion, that is by the prospect of reward, seems to me to be fundamental.

If you look around our own country and think of the great productive concerns which have been built up in it in the last generation—vast enterprises like the iron and steel industry, the machinery industry, the textile industry, giving employment to many thousands and providing the essential condition of our defence and security in this war—and then ask yourselves whether you really believe that these results would have been got under a system of State ownership and control, you will, I am sure, admit that private enterprise, while it must not be allowed to become our master, has been a magnificent servant and can do vital things for us in the future.

The second of my conclusions is that, in envisaging the future world after the war, we should not seek to destroy this driving progressive element which really represents one of the deep-seated instincts of man, but should seek to control and direct it in the interests of the people as a whole. In other words, the choice is not between an unrestricted capitalism and a universal socialism. We shall do much better if we keep the good elements of the capitalist system, while at the same time imposing upon capital the most stringent obligations to discharge its social and industrial duty.

The old conservative doctrine that the function of the State was merely to keep the ring for the combatants has gone for ever. The grim picture, dear to the heart of the Yarra Bank orator, of a capitalist system in which there is unrestrained and cruel competition, in which employees are sweated and workers treated like cattle, no doubt had some truth in it—and still has too much to satisfy humane minds. But we have learned a great deal about how to use private enterprise for our own social and national ends. Price control and Government regulation have been limiting factors. Arbitration courts and industrial laws have abolished sweating, except in one or two places where the award-evader has yet to be chased out of his burrow. National insurance, our unsuccessful attempt at which, just before the war, was most disappointing to many and caused my own resignation from a cabinet, must come again. As early as may be, and if possible during the war when employment is high, unemployment insurance should be introduced. After the war, the obligation of industry to maintain employment on a steadier basis must be increased to the limits of practicability; we must become better economists in our attack upon the problem of boom and depression; we must aim at a proper provision of food, clothing and shelter for our citizens. In these and many other ways the duty of each of us to his fellows and to the State must be defined and enforced.

But however elaborate the machine, it must have a motive power, a driving force. And in a material sense that force, I repeat, must be the urge in the human being to strive for progress and for reward—the instinct to get his own private property, to make his own savings, to earn his own independent future. The great race of men is that one in which each individual develops his fullest individuality, in which ambition is encouraged, in which there are rewards for the courageous and enterprising, in which there is no foolish doctrine of equality between the active and the idle, the intelligent and the dull, the frugal and the improvident.

A modern and civilized capitalism has much to contribute to the post-war world.

7 *August, 1942.*

XXII

THE DRINK PROBLEM

RECENTLY a great deal of discussion has been occurring both in Parliament and Press in Melbourne, and perhaps elsewhere, in relation to the undoubted abuses of intoxicants which are taking place in the large centres of population.

Unfortunately, as it seems to me, a great deal of the debate has been made up of allegations and of charges and counter-charges, some of them probably of an extravagant kind. The heat which results tends to obscure the real problem.

It is true that the licensing laws of the nation have been and are controlled by State Parliaments and administered by State Executives. But the Commonwealth, in time of war, has certain responsibilities which it cannot escape, and has within its power certain courses of action which, in my opinion, would come nearer to the root of these troubles than most of the suggestions that have been made.

To me the outstanding fact is that three years ago drunkenness was diminishing in Australia, the standard of hotels was being raised, and the general public attitude was pretty accurately shown by the fact that in my own State, for example, the no-licence vote receded. In other words, public opinion, so far as one can judge it, was not acutely dissatisfied with the character or administration of the licensing laws.

To-day, after three years of war, there can I think be no doubt that there is acute public dissatisfaction and an insistent demand for reform.

This short history surely demonstrates that the war is responsible for those additional causes which have produced additional and noticeable abuses.

What are these causes? Personally, I do not believe that they are to be found in a sudden degeneration of the character of the average citizen. It is true that the ultimate cure for the abuse of drink is to be found in the character of the individual and his capacity for moderation and self-restraint, self-discipline. But to state this is to state an ideal, and not to grapple with the immediate problem.

If, then, I am right in saying that the national character has not suddenly degenerated, what is the reason for this quite sudden development of excessive drinking, particularly in the capitals? No doubt it can be to a substantial degree attributed to wartime social conditions.

Men of the fighting services come home on a few days' leave; somewhat foolish notions of entertainment prevail, and the result is that the consumption of drink goes up. Standards all round are a little loosened, and the community becomes a little more noisy, so to speak, in its habits.

But, having said all that, we have still not reached what I believe to be the fundamental cause of the trouble. The fundamental cause (apart, of course, from the defects of human nature) is in my opinion to be found in two associated facts. One is that the very substantial increase in the national income as a result of war expenditure is being steadily diverted from essential commodities—which are increasingly in relatively short supply—to luxury commodities, one of the principal of which is drink.

If you increase the wages bill of a country like this by something of the order of £150,000,000 a year and take no adequate steps to draw off for purposes of war a substantial proportion of the added purchasing power and if, at the same time, you ration clothing, tea, sugar and other commodities, you must expect that people will have more cash in their pockets and that, having more cash and being normal and comparatively unthinking people, they will buy two drinks instead of one, or three drinks instead of two.

There is a second cause, directly related to the first. It is that the reduction in the total supply of liquor has been relatively small, while there has been no reduction whatever in the number of places licensed to sell it. If you bring into conjunction very large supplies of liquor and very large sums of spare spending money it is quite inevitable that you will have an increase in drinking and an increase in drunkenness.

To seek to cure such a problem by ignoring these root causes and talking merely in terms of stricter penalties or more police, desirable as these latter things may be, is to miss the whole point of the contest.

I speak to you about this matter from the point of view of a man who is, like many of you, neither a teetotaller nor an addict. My chief objective has always been the prevention or abolition of privileges for any class of business. For the life of me I cannot understand why the quite legitimate and useful hotel business should be any more immune from the impact of war conditions than the quite legitimate and useful business of selling sugar or tea or sardines.

We have heard a great deal about the rationalization of industry. We know that many hundreds if not thousands of small shops and businesses have been compelled to close, and that hundreds of branches of banks have been forced to close. We know there has been a very substantial reduction in the consumption of newsprint, of paper for wrappings; that the whole position of clothing supply has been revolutionized and the quantity of clothing for sale reduced. We know that all these and a hundred other things have taken place.

All that I ask, as a plain and sensible citizen, is why it should be thought that some rule applies to the selling of beer which does not apply to the carrying on of banking, or why tailors and shopkeepers should be asked to accept losses, and sometimes abolition, while those who sell the things we drink go relatively free except for some mild—very mild—reduction in the quantity of their turnover.

My view, then, can be summed up in two propositions: First, that we shall be playing with this problem, which is essentially one of dangerous extravagance with deplorable social results, unless and until we attack extravagance by diminishing the capacity of people to be extravagant; which means that there must be a far more thorough-going diversion of spending power to real war needs than any we are now witnessing.

Austerity campaigns are insufficient because, if experience counts for anything, they will succeed with the austere and leave the irresponsible and the extravagant unmoved. There must be a compulsion to frugality, and when we have frugality, intemperance and extravagance will automatically be subdued.

The second proposition is that, both in point of the rationalization of industry and the reduction of goods available for sale, there is no earthly reason why the Australian liquor trade should not be required to submit to the controls and limitations that we quite cheerfully impose upon other and very frequently much more useful civil industries.

In brief, we have here a most important economic and social problem, which ought to be dealt with on its merits, without wild talk and certainly without fear, favour or affection.

4 September, 1942.

I

XXIII

IS INFLATION A BOGEY?

Very few people ever learn from the experience of others. It
seems to be one of the laws of life that, whatever misfortunes
may have happened to others as a result of certain policies or
circumstances, we still hug to ourselves the delusion that it
cannot happen to us.

It is no doubt for this reason that most Australians appear
to be comparatively unmoved by the thought of currency inflation. It is safe to say that they are not unmoved in Germany
where, up to the time of the war at any rate, and no doubt
during it, constant safeguards against inflation were adopted by
those in financial control. But then of course Germany knows
what inflation means, having been bankrupted by it some years
after the last war.

The French people know all about it, having in modern
times seen the franc fall in value from about a shilling to, at
one stage, about a penny.

Mammoth British financial efforts in this war have been conducted with due regard to the avoidance of inflation, for the
British people were sufficiently near to France and Germany to
know almost at first hand what a ruinous and devastating thing
inflation can be.

We read from time to time in the financial journals of the
sustained effort in the United States to avoid inflationary finance;
and this is not to be wondered at, for during the civil war

millions of American citizens got to know to their own cost what depreciation of the currency could do to them.

Are we awake to these matters in Australia, or must we learn from our own bitter experience?

Broadly speaking, inflation occurs when the supply of purchasing power outruns the supply of goods and services to be bought, with the result that costs and prices are forced up and the value of the pound is correspondingly reduced.

An understanding of the problem depends essentially upon getting to appreciate one central fact, which is that a pound note is intrinsically worth only the paper and ink used in its manufacture, and that its real value is expressed purely in terms of what it will buy.

If in the course of the next twelve months prices in Australia rose one hundred per cent, that would be merely another way of saying that the value of the pound had been reduced by fifty per cent, £1 at the end of the year being needed to buy what 10/- would have bought at the beginning of the year. In other words, inflation of the currency means devaluation of the pound.

It was admirably described once in my presence as "a flat rate tax upon everybody's pound note, whether the owner of the pound note is rich or poor." So the first point to be observed about inflation is that it is inequitable taxation, since it is imposed upon everybody at the same rate.

The second thing to be noted about it is that, by reducing the value of money, it reduces the value of money claims such as savings, bank credits, insurance policies, investments on mortgage, preference shares and the like. Competent observers have contended that the German inflation after the last war practically wiped out the middle classes, and thereby paved the way for the rise of national socialism.

I have had occasion before to say something to you about the damaging effect of too many of our policies on those thrifty and frugal people who are the backbone of the nation. What I want to point out to you to-night is that these are of all people the ones who would be most grievously injured by inflation.

My experience suggests that some big business men are indifferent to the danger of inflation. I think I understand some of their reasons, and I shall not take up your time to-night by discussing them, except to say that great wealth and selfishness are not always strangers to one another.

At the other end of the financial scale one finds many thousands of wage-earners who appear to think that inflation will not touch them, because, they say, inflation will raise prices and therefore the cost of living, and their wages will be adjusted to the cost of living, so that in effect nominal wages will rise and the wage-earner will still be safe.

Let me say quite plainly that this is a most dangerous illusion. Once inflation really gets going and the price level really begins to go up quickly, no periodic adjustment of wages will ever catch it up.

Continental experience showed that, when the full effect of inflation became felt, adjustments in the value of money were taking place weekly, and then daily and then hourly. You just cannot adjust wages as rapidly as that, and consequently—as the German wage-earner discovered—the worker's pay is overwhelmed by the price level, and he is involved in the same ruin as the other people in the community.

Now, to all this some wise man will reply, "Oh, yes, inflation got out of hand in Germany, but we know better; we know how to handle these things."

Well, do we? I should be very surprised to learn that the leading financiers of Germany in the last twenty years were any less competent than the leading financiers of Australia. The truth is that real inflation—I am not talking of some strictly limited use of credit and currency expansion—is in its nature almost impossible to control. It grows, so to speak, on itself.

A Government, in order to provide for its expenditure, may rely upon taxation, public loans and central bank credit. For political reasons it comes to the conclusion that it is unwilling to tax beyond a certain point, and unlikely successfully to borrow beyond a certain point. It then turns to the central bank and says, "All right, you must find the difference." In the case of the present Commonwealth budget that difference may very well be a staggering sum of the order of £200,000,000.

Such a volume of central bank credit must, on the view of any expert in this country, produce marked inflation, and do it on an already inflated foundation, for I remind you that the Commonwealth note issue, which was a shade under £50,000,000 when the war began, is now itself £110,000,000, and the central bank credit used last financial year and unprovided for in this budget was not less than £80,000,000.

When inflation takes effect prices rise, costs rise and wages, though more slowly, rise also. The result is that the cost of all defence works is increased. The result of that is that the deficit is increased. The result of that is that, to meet the deficit, still more central bank credit has to be obtained. The result of that is further inflation. The result of that is further increases in prices and costs, further deficits, further borrowing, further inflation, the whole thing proceeding in a spiral which inevitably mounts upon itself until it touches the skies.

The only real answer to the inflation danger is to divert purchasing power from the citizen to the Government. Our resources must more and more be spent on the war, and not on civil goods or services. Our civil consumption must be taxed down, borrowed down, and rationed down.

Some of us think that compulsory borrowing would in the long run be the best thing for most of us, because it would reduce civil spending, be a great check upon inflation, and at the same time provide a sort of readjustment fund for hundreds of thousands when the war is over.

But let us avoid inflation at almost any cost, for it may be a pleasant drug while war is on, but its reaction is disastrous.

11 September, 1942.

XXIV

COMPULSORY UNIONISM

RECENTLY there has been a good deal of discussion about compulsory unionism. Indeed, there is some evidence that the Government has been taking some steps towards making it a working principle in the case of Government contracts. It is therefore necessary that you and I should have some clear and reasoned view about it.

I happen to be against it. But my opposition to it is not an opposition to unionism as such. The trades union movement has meant a great deal in our industrial history. It has represented collective bargaining. It has given strength to the workers as a group which no worker as an individual could have possessed. It has been an effective weapon against the obdurate or short-sighted employer. It has had supreme value in the working of the characteristically Australian system of compulsory industrial arbitration. As a servant of the wage-earner, unionism has done an extraordinarily good job of work.

The movement for compulsory unionism breaks new ground. The trades union has been a splendid servant. It now aspires to be a master.

Some weeks ago I made a series of broadcasts on what I called "President Roosevelt's Four Freedoms". But there was one freedom to which the President did not refer—freedom of association.

It will perhaps be one of the ironies of history that the trades union movement which, in the days of the famous Tolpuddle martyrs, represented a struggle for freedom of industrial association, should now have taken a new turn so that it desires not that there should be freedom to associate in a trades union but that there should be no freedom not to associate in a trades union.

Freedom of association is of the first order of importance in the world of liberty. It is important that I should be free to associate with other people who think as I do. It is not always realized that it is equally important that I should be free not to associate with people who do not think as I do. That philosophic point of view is the first argument against compulsory unionism.

But the second ground on which it is to be attacked is that it is undemocratic. The essence of democracy is freedom. The denial of democracy is fascism. The whole principle of the fascist movement is authority, and the authoritarian principle of government is at the poles from the democratic principle of government.

When Mussolini set up the dictator system in Italy, he did it on the foundation of a series of lesser authorities exercised by unions and associations. He realized that the great enemy of autocratic authority is the lively minority, and he therefore determined that minorities should not count, and that the law of the majority should be a tyrant's law. Make no mistake. It is true, as wise men have said for a hundred years, that the real test of liberty in any country is the way in which minorities are treated.

Now, let us turn to another aspect of this matter. In Australia the organization of the Australian Labour Party as a party political force is founded upon the organization of the trades unions, affiliated with the trades hall. If my son is by compulsion a member of a trades union in a craft or occupation that he practises, then, willynilly, he is a subscriber to those political funds through which the Labour Party conducts its political campaign. I shall never forget one of my friends and colleagues in the Federal Parliament, who is a prominent public accountant, telling me with a wry smile that, compulsory unionism being the law in his State, his two sons who were employed in his business had the privilege of subscribing to the support of the Labour candidate who was standing against him at the next election.

Whatever may be the position in other countries, the trades union movement is in Australia the backbone of the Labour movement. It has great funds and great influence. Its militant sections make no secret of the fact that they are out to secure union control of the actual conduct of Australian industries. This means, if we are to give up the blind use of parrot cries and really endeavour to understand what they mean, that trades unionism is rapidly becoming a great vested interest in Australia—a vested interest just as powerful as that of any manufacturing cartel and, what is important at present, the only one to add immensely to its strength during the war.

What sort of a vested interest will the trades union movement become if it has a compelled and universal membership; if, as at present, it pays no income tax on its revenues; if, by reason of reserved occupations, its full-time officials are protected from the military duties of war; if, as we have seen, it makes its wartime concessions only for compensation in the form of cash; and if, as our political history has shown, it has determined that Parliament shall dance to its tune and obey its law?

Now, when I say all these things I am getting down to a pretty fundamental issue of our time. If there is one thing that distinguishes the democratic system from the dictatorship system, it is that in our own casual and cheerful fashion we do believe in liberty. If you cross-examine any one of us about what he believes, you will probably discover that in the last resort he dislikes interference and believes that, within decent limits, he should be allowed to live his own life in his own way, provided that he does not injure his neighbour, performs his social duty, and is honest and fair in the performance of his community duty.

Liberty, as I was at some pains to point out in my talks to you on the four freedoms, is not only liberty to do something, but also liberty *not* to do something. Freedom of worship must involve freedom not to worship; freedom of thought must involve freedom not to think as others do; freedom to associate with Jones and Brown must involve freedom not to associate with Jones and Brown.

It is merely our reluctance to go beneath the surface that makes us toy with the idea of compulsory unionism. We say, "Oh well, unionism has been a good thing for the worker; it has got him, sometimes against the opposition of stupid employers, better wages and better conditions; and it is absurd that people who are not unionists should get the benefit of these things when they have not accepted a share of the burden of getting them." But, plausible as this may be, it will still be true that the Australian trades union, for the most part, is not only an industrial but a political organism. What would the average Australian say if he were told to-morrow that financial membership of the United Australia Party or the Country Party had been made compulsory? He would complain to high heaven. Is there any less reason why he should complain if, by compulsion, he is made a member of an organization some portion of his contributions to which is used for the support of the political Labour Party?

There have been some interesting recent developments in this movement for compulsion. There is a good deal of evidence to show that the Government, through its contracting departments, has been requiring that contractors should employ only union labour. There is also a good deal of evidence that certain departments of the Government have been laying down the rule that, where awards are obtained, only those who belong to trades unions shall enjoy their benefit.

As a lawyer with considerable experience in industrial law, I know that technically the benefit of Arbitration Court awards is enforceable only by members of registered organizations. But it is a new doctrine that a Government which owes a responsibility to everybody—unionist and non-unionist alike—will discriminate in its payments between those who are unionists and those who are not.

Recently I spoke to you about the function and value of the capitalist system, about the value of individual initiative, not only in the preserving of the world that we now know, but in the building up of a prosperous new order which will give us strength and security in the future. The whole essence of my case was that you get the best community results when you encourage the best individual results: that you get the best sort of thing for the nation when, within proper limits of decency, you encourage the individual to get the best kind of thing for himself.

Can all this square with a system in which all employed citizens are, whether they like it or not, dragooned into highly political industrial organizations and are taught to believe that the individual does not count?

As democrats we have many times in my own life been disturbed by the disposition of so many people to pass their individual responsibility on to somebody else's shoulders—by the temptation that comes to every man to say, "What does it matter what I do or do not do? Somebody else will attend to it for me." But we have not always been so clearly conscious of the fact that true democracy requires that the individual should think for himself, suffer for himself, act and vote according to his own judgment and on his own responsibility. If this is, as I most profoundly believe it to be, a war for all the rights of democratic man, it must mean that what we are struggling for is the right of every human soul—which is also an immortal soul—to reach its full development. What you must ask yourselves is whether that development will reach its peak under a system in which men are regimented and controlled merely because they practise some craft or follow some occupation in common.

We all, at once, concede that it would be monstrous to compel people to be Catholic or Protestant, Anglican or Presbyterian, according to the will of the majority; that we should compel people to be Liberal or Conservative, according to the will of the majority. Is it any more absurd that we should adopt a system which compels people to be the industrial supporters or financial subsidizers of some political party, according to the will of the majority?

A few weeks ago I listened to a Scots Presbyterian preacher who had some good things to say to the effect that the world's progress had never depended upon ideas produced by the majority, but had always depended upon the burning faith of a relatively few men. That is something worth thinking about.

It is perhaps not untrue to say that if, in the history of the last hundred years, everybody had been compelled to subscribe to what the majority thought, there would have been no progress in the world and we should have become merely a community of dumb and driven cattle.

14 August, 1942.

XXV

THE FUNCTION OF THE OPPOSITION
IN PARLIAMENT

EVERY now and then you will read an allegation by somebody
to the effect that the Opposition is "playing party politics" or
that some individual member of the Opposition is open to
criticism because he has criticized or attacked some aspect of
Government policy or administration.

We are urged to pull together, apparently on the assumption
that once a war comes upon us we should all think exactly
the same way about all our problems. This kind of criticism
seems to me to exhibit a confusion of thought which requires
a few minutes' quiet and dispassionate examination.

What is the function of the Opposition and its members at a
time like this?

You will remember that in Australia we do not have, as they
have in Great Britain, an all-party administration. I need not
go into the history of the reasons for this, because you are no
doubt familiar with them. But the fact remains that we have a
purely party Government, with its inevitable consequence, a
purely party Opposition. In other words we are, in Parliament,
divided on party lines.

The present Government has always maintained, even when
it was in opposition, that this is the proper way of constituting
Parliament, notwithstanding the war, and I have no desire at
this stage to debate it. I merely accept it as the fact.

Now, what are the consequences of this? The first and greatest is that you cannot maintain the party system of government and at the same time expect the Opposition to treat the Government as if it were an all-party Government. In all-party Government differences of opinion must inevitably arise between individual ministers, but they are ironed out in the Cabinet Room, and the result, while it might not fully express the views of any individual, will represent what we call the "corporate wisdom" of the Cabinet.

In a party system of government there is no joint cabinet in which differences may be ironed out, and therefore those differences must be discussed frankly and fully in Parliament so that Parliament itself may arrive at its own ultimate conclusion as to what is the wise thing to do.

It follows from this that the function of an Opposition is to be quite unhesitating in its willingness to debate large matters of policy, to criticize the Government views on those matters, to put forward and maintain its own. Only in this way will Parliament serve its function of giving expression to contending opinions, which in fact exist in the community.

This does not mean that we are to behave as if there were no war on. In time of peace it is legitimate and proper to debate all your differences, great and small, but in war trivial matters must clearly be put aside. The great thing that we have to remember in days like these is that we have a common danger —a danger which touches and concerns every one of us, whatever his political views or economic position—and a common aim which is, among other things, to enable free parliamentary institutions to continue in this country when the war is over. It follows from this that whatever the party alignments may be in Parliament, we must be prepared to suppress or forget all differences which would weaken the war effort.

You will see, however, that this does not mean that, because there is a war and our position is critical, Parliament is to be conducted as if the Opposition were not present or, being present, were devoid of ideas and incapable of speech. If Parliament is to be a collection of what our American friends call "yes-men", then it will become uncommonly like some European Parliaments, and might as well not sit.

If a member of the Opposition expounds his view on an important public question on which he has the misfortune to differ from the Government, it is foolish simply to say "party politics", when that is our system of government. In any case, the members of the Opposition believe that their ideas are right and good just as our opponents belonging to the Labour Party believe that Labour ideas are right and good. To seek to prevent either side from having its own ideas is to exhibit a distrust of parliamentary government instead of a realization that it is, or should be, one of the real sources of our strength.

So, as I see it, the Opposition has certain duties and rights. As a body of patriotic men, it is bound to co-operate by being willing to accept joint responsibility for unpopular but necessary measures. It would be scandalous to endeavour to make political capital out of something the Government was doing in the best interests of winning the war.

But there is a converse side to all this. Just as it would be scandalous to oppose necessary and good measures, so it would be weak and irresponsible to refuse to oppose strongly any measures that the Opposition regarded as nationally unsound. On some great matters of debate we may think, and do think, strongly that we are right. Our opponents equally strongly think that they are right. It is only by the frankest and most manly exchange of argument that the truth will ever be ascertained.

As an Opposition, therefore, we must be willing not only to oppose what we think wrong but to suggest those things that we think ought to be done. We have a constructive function, and because of that we must avoid mere sectional argument and barren debating points.

Take the questions that arise in connexion with domestic or internal policy during a war. The people of this country have always been sharply divided about them. If, because of the gravity of the war position, our various views on domestic policy are to be put on one side—if partisan arguments about them are to be abandoned all round—well and good. But it is ludicrous to suggest that they should be maintained on one side and abandoned on the other.

As an individual I happen to have strong views, developed by study and experience over a number of years, on such questions as socialization, public finance and the encouragement of enterprise. I have no desire to go on discussing these matters at a time like this just for the sake of discussing them. But if I honestly come to the conclusion that domestic policies are being pursued which run counter to my beliefs on these matters and which therefore, from my point of view, are damaging to the best interests of Australia, it is my plain duty to speak up clearly and unambiguously about them.

What we occasionally forget is that, while we are all agreed upon the supreme necessity of concentrating the national effort on the war, there is always room for marked difference of opinion as to how that concentration can be best effected.

One of my friends on the other side of the House may say, "I believe that we can get the best concentration of effort by having the Government take over industries." All right. But if I believe that for the Government to take over the industries of the nation will hinder and not help the war effort, am I to be silent just because some onlooker accuses me of party-consciousness?

We must have realism on these questions, and we shall get it to the greatest possible extent if we make up our minds that in politics to-day we shall debate only those things which are of really national importance, and that when we have our debates we shall conduct ourselves with a proper mixture of vigour, courtesy and good sense.

8 May, 1942.

K

XXVI

THE OPPOSITION'S DUTY

In May last I took the opportunity in one of my broadcasts of discussing what seemed to me the function of the Opposition in the Federal political structure.

Recently this topic has come under active public discussion because certain public criticisms made by the Opposition through its leader have given rise to an exhibition of resentment in Government circles and even to threats of an immediate election. It is therefore appropriate that I should once more state what I believe to be the true principle which must determine the Opposition's conduct and mark out its duty.

There is in Australia no all-party administration. For better or for worse the present Government, when in Opposition and continually since, has made it clear that it does not believe in an all-party government; that, on the contrary, it believes that even under present circumstances there should be a party administration acting through the ordinary party machinery and giving effect to party policy.

The inevitable result of this is that there must be a party Opposition. We Australians have a deep-rooted and sound instinct against anybody being allowed to have things both ways, and there will be little public sympathy for an opinion which says that, while there is to be a purely one-party administration on the treasury benches, there is at the same time to be a non-party Opposition.

It is, I believe, a grave misfortune for Australia that party politics should not have been suspended for the duration of the war; but it is a misfortune for which the Opposition cannot accept responsibility, and for which you will agree that I myself who, when Prime Minister, offered to stand down and serve under a Labour Prime Minister, can accept no shadow of responsibility.

The Opposition, then, being forced to be a party Opposition, has had to consider its duty. In its view, with which I think you will agree, its duty falls into two parts: First, on the positive side, it must constructively help in the carrying out of all measures, however unpopular, which truly relate to the marshalling and use of the country's resources for the prosecution of the war to a complete success. Second, on the negative side, it must oppose by every means within its command any use of the war powers for purely partisan domestic ends, and criticize within the limits of national security any acts it believes to represent erroneous or harmful administration.

Just turn your mind back for a few weeks and recall the chief matters upon which the Opposition has voiced criticisms. They have been: The Government's proposed four per cent profit limitation, the failure to convert the Australian army into one army with the same conditions of service, compulsory unionism, certain censorship matters, and the Government's handling of the man power problem.

Was it improper to criticize the four per cent proposals? It can hardly lie in the mouth of the Government to say so, because the outstanding result of the criticism made was that the Government admitted their force and publicly announced that it was abandoning the proposals.

Then take the question of one army. Here is a matter of first-class importance to Australia, particularly if we are, at a suitable time and under suitable military circumstances, to conduct an

offensive. Are we really to be told that the Opposition in Parliament, though it may have the strongest views on such a question,
is to suppress them? Why, you might as well abolish the
Opposition altogether and say that, for the rest of the war, the
Executive is to govern Australia without reference to Parliament
and unaffected by any public opinion which has had—what
every public opinion needs—a fair and full statement of both
sides.

To be a member of Parliament at a time like this and to be
compelled to be silent about matters of first-class importance in
Australia's war effort would be a position intolerable to a self-
respecting man. It is one that I could not myself accept for a
moment.

Then there is compulsory unionism. Recently I had the opportunity of making a broadcast to you about it. Was the making
of such a broadcast an improper thing? Am I or are you, because
there is a war on, to sit silently and allow freedom of industrial
association to disappear, perhaps for ever?

Is censorship, to take the fourth matter I have mentioned,
to be not only authoritative, which I agree it should be, but
also placed beyond criticism? If it is, then opinion in this country
will cease to be the product of the exercise by each of us of an
immemorial privilege, and will come under complete control.

My last example was man power. Here we have a question
which is at the very root of our national effort. Australia has not
an unlimited population or unlimited resources. She is bound
in this war to do absolutely everything she can to play her full
part. But what is her full part? It is one in which the greatest
practicable number of fighting men are adequately trained and
adequately equipped for modern war, while production and distribution are sufficiently carried on to attend to the needs of the
services, munitions, the civil population and certain essential

exports of foodstuffs and material to our allies, notably Great
Britain.

In other words, the problem of man power is not a question
merely of adding up the maximum demands of the services
and of munitions and then subtracting the necessary power
from the rest of the community; it is essentially a problem
of scientific balance, and of so apportioning our resources
that each vital element gets as fair and as full a share as is
practicable.

Is the mere fact that one or two ministers are put in charge of
these matters to close the mouths of all the rest of us? Is an
Opposition bound to be silent if it honestly believes that blunders
are being made, that maladjustment is resulting, that unnecessary
shortages are being imposed upon people because the man-
power problem has got out of balance?

You see, it is not a question of the Government saying to the
Opposition, "You are wrong in your arguments, and therefore
you must not say what you in fact say." Who is to determine
whether the Opposition is right or wrong? Obviously not the
Government but, in the long run, public opinion. The whole
essence of the parliamentary system is that we get at the truth
by the process of debate, by the process of educating our minds
and judgments by the hearing of reasoned arguments on both
sides.

I notice that certain correspondents, writing to the newspapers,
are disposed to dismiss all this argument as if it were irresponsible wrangling in the face of the enemy. But we must think
calmly and clearly about this matter.

Personal abuse is one thing; to sensible people it rarely does
more than condemn the man who engages in it. But honest
argument about important questions is quite another; and the
argument does not become any the less honest or important

because it is expressed and pursued with vigour and determination.

I have a very clear recollection that for the first two years of this war, when I was myself Prime Minister, there was no lack of criticism and discussion. A great deal of it was engaged in by some of those who now seek to tell us that a wartime Government should be above criticism and beyond debate. Has criticism come to an end in Great Britain or in the United States? You have only to read your cables to know that it has not. In the House of Commons they still enjoy full liberty to say what they think of the Government or of any minister. It is only in Germany and Italy that this democratic privilege no longer exists.

And has the criticism in Great Britain been dangerous or useless? The fact is that it has, since the war began, produced one major change of Government, a great number of changes in Government personnel, and from time to time considerable alterations of policy. All this is to the good.

When I was in office I used to hear loud demands from those on the other side of Parliament that Parliament should sit more frequently and for longer periods. Why was this? Was it so that the Opposition could practise uttering a concerted "yes" to everything the Government put forward, or was it in order that Parliament should perform its proper function—not of being mischievous or irresponsible, but of soberly and strongly debating the conduct of the war and of our external and domestic policies?

I tell you, listeners, that it will be a black day for self-governing freedom in Australia when to be a political critic is considered improper, or when the only criticism permitted is one couched in mild and apologetic terms.

In time of war in a country like this no word is to be spoken which will give information to the enemy or which will assist him to conduct his war against us. No wild and offensive statements are to be made which will divide the people on immaterial grounds. Of all action justly and necessarily taken by any Government, no Opposition should seek to take party advantage. But within these limits I maintain and will continue to maintain that, where you have a party Government, a party Opposition has a duty not merely to itself but, much more importantly, to the people, which it is bound to discharge fearlessly and persistently.

28 August, 1942.

XXVII

THE GOVERNMENT AND OURSELVES

IT is one of the ironies of our democratic system that, while its essence is that Government is self-government, so that what we call the Government is ourselves and nobody else, most of us go on as if the Government were something remote and even hostile.

In a democracy, if we take the average for a term of years and omit the short and perhaps accidental periods, the Government—whatever its party colour—is something we have ourselves set up. Its policy is broadly the policy of a majority of us. Its members are drawn from a majority of those whom we, as electors, have freely chosen.

These seem simple truths, but they are commonly forgotten. So is the great truth that there can be no true and effective democracy unless there is an identity of interest and responsibility and duty between the elected and the elector.

Apply these principles to the individual voter. If he truly understands his democratic duty he will live in the constant recollection of his identity with the Government, and his actions will be governed by that fact. He will protect its interests because he will know that they are his. He will pay his taxes without evasion because he will know that the punctual observance of each democrat's duty to the State is the only real source of the State's strength. He will do his work in the munitions factory, at a time like this, not merely for a special war bonus or profit, but also because he will see it as his democratic contribution to a democratic war.

But if our democrat does not understand his duty he will—in common with, unhappily, far too many of us—think of the Government, as a correspondent of mine puts it, as "that remote, somewhat godlike power which is the bestower of benefits, and the scapegoat which bears the sinful burden of everybody's failures."

Here we touch upon one of the great maladies of democracy—a malady which can easily become malignant and destroy us: that rather futile and supine acceptance of the idle and false doctrine that the Government owes us everything while we owe the Government nothing.

Let us be clear about this: that to be a real democrat in a really democratic country is to occupy a position of great dignity and self-respect, for these qualities are the natural and proper attributes of independent man. To be one of those who mouth the catch-cries of democracy and stridently clamour for their so-called "rights" from the cradle to the grave and after it, but at the same time dodge every civic responsibility, is to occupy a position not of dignity but of contempt.

If I see the State as a grouping of you and me and millions like us, retaining our individuality but seeking strength in unity, I shall not need to be told that to rob the State is to rob myself; that to betray the State is to betray myself; that to become grumbling or cunningly hostile to the State is to start a civil war in my own household.

There are plenty of poor democrats in this country. Let me identify two examples of them. First, there is the tax-evader. Large incomes are to-day taxed to the very limit. The large-scale war profiteer, if returns are accurately made, is a sheer impossibility; a tax of 18/- in the pound soon sweats it out of him. We are spending a third of our total of individual incomes on war. Yet the orgy of profuse spending and luxurious living is not ended. When we look about us it is hard to believe that there are not many people who evade the law and think it clever. They are not only poor democrats; there is no real room for them in a democratic country. Again, there is the absentee worker—far too many of him; a small fraction of the working population, it is true, but too many when there is a war on and coal or shells lost are a treasonable gift to the enemy.

The war striker; the war absentee; the war profiteer-maker—these are all bad democrats, and all their vociferous lip service to democracy will not amend that fact.

Let me carry this a little farther and be quite direct about it. Let us consider one feature of our war set-up which must occasionally give us furiously to think, if it does not actually move us to shame. The Australian who to-day wants to evade paying a tax, whatever the amount of his income, is a poor Australian, for he is not prepared to fight, even safely, with his money for Australian democracy.

Seventy per cent of the total of all earned incomes in Australia is earned by people with under £8 per week—a seventy per cent which totals around £600,000,000. It is this vast sum which provides the great bulk of the purchasing power in the shops and markets of Australia. Yet it pays only a few millions towards the war.

"Oh," I am told, "you can't ask the wage-earner not only to work long hours but in addition to pay a tax on what he earns in those long hours."

Why not, indeed? The man who has enlisted in the armed forces has, in many thousands of cases, reduced his earnings, has taxed himself by a half, by two-thirds, by three-quarters. His hours are unlimited; he has no overtime pay, no war loading

—except the loading of imminent peril of his life. If *he* can pay those taxes and sustain this sacrifice, how can the munition-worker or any other of us civilians hope to avoid at least some fraction of it?

Of course, the answer is that ninety per cent of munition-workers, in common with ninety per cent of wage-earners throughout Australia, do not want to avoid it. They are good citizens and good democrats. But the ten per cent of poor democrats are vocal. Indeed, I almost come to believe that a good democrat is one with a silent acceptance of his duty, while a bad democrat is one with a noisy insistence upon his rights.

It all comes back to the sense of responsibility—that quiet and lovely virtue which can convert seven millions of individual people into a good and faithful community.

The spirit we need is the spirit of the enlisted men and women in time of war; the spirit of sturdy independence of the great middle class at all times; of the people who save, who are frugal, who take out insurance policies, who yearn for and maintain education, who stand on their own feet and pay above and beyond all this for the assistance of others.

A French king once said, "L'état, c'est moi." ("The State, it is myself.") In his mouth it was the expression of despotism. In the mouths of a million people it could become the very expression of democracy.

5 June, 1942.

XXVIII

SEA POWER

THE influence of sea power on British history has been profound. That a small island in the North Sea, about the size of the State of Victoria, should in the days of Elizabeth, with a population substantially less than that of Australia to-day, have taken the first momentous steps in a great movement which in two hundred years was to put a ring of colonies around the world seems miraculous, until you remember that this achievement was mainly due to the mariners of England.

The story of British expansion is primarily linked with the names of sailormen—of Raleigh, Drake, Frobisher, Cook, Nelson.

> We sailed wherever ships could sail.
> We founded many a mighty state.

Our sea power has won our modern wars for us. It has in turn defeated Spain and Holland and France and Germany.

Earlier in the present war it became the fashion to dismiss sea power as something outmoded and to concentrate all attention on the air. I shall be the last to minimize the heroism, the efforts, or the importance of the air force. But extreme views are very seldom correct, and we now find ourselves coming back to a balanced judgment which shows that those who thought about these things before the war were not a mile out when they decided that all three arms must be brought up to a reasonable degree of co-ordinated preparedness.

But tonight I want to emphasize to you the importance of the sea - not its diminishing importance, but its growing importance.

I believe that it can be established that some of our major setbacks in this war have been caused by our failure to maintain sea power, and that ultimate victory in the war depends upon sea power to a most astonishing extent.

Let me make two things clear. The first is that by sea power I mean strength in both naval and merchant shipping. The second is that I regard as an essential ingredient in any modern fleet a large provision of aircraft carriers and of naval aircraft, since it is abundantly plain that large ships without spotting and bombing and fighting aircraft would be as great an anomaly as large ships without long-range guns.

I said just now that some of our reverses were due to our failure to maintain sea power. For an example of this we do not need to go very far from home. Can anybody doubt that the terrible blow delivered to the American fleet at Pearl Harbour and the sinking of our own battleships in the Gulf of Siam gave to Japan in the Western Pacific a degree of naval superiority which made it easy for her to invade Malaya, the Philippines, the Netherlands East Indies, Rabaul, New Guinea, and which was beyond question the biggest factor in Japan's swift success?

I know that somebody will retort to this that it was Japanese air power that did it, but my reply is to point out that it was the Japanese naval air arm which attacked Pearl Harbour and sank our battleships, and that without naval supremacy in these Far Eastern waters Japanese land-based aircraft might never have been able to establish themselves, with military forces to defend them, in key strategic points.

Let us look farther afield and glance briefly at the future.

Wherever we look we will see that the great problem is shipping —sea power and shipping: numbers of ships, tonnage of ships, quick loading of ships, quick work and turn-around in ports, the protection of ships against the enemy in the air and on the water and under the water.

Great Britain must be fed and supplied, not only as the last stronghold of resistance on the west coast of Europe, but as the vital spearhead for the counter-attack which must precede victory. She can be fed and supplied only by sea, and the great and continuing and bitter battle of the Atlantic is therefore not only her vital struggle but that of the world.

Russia must be aided. The only way in which direct aid can be sent into Russia is by water, and the sinking of many a British merchant ship and warship engaged in the dangerous and indeed deadly task of helping Russia is the best proof of the importance which attaches to it.

Take the other method of helping Russia so much advocated today —the opening of a second front. The biggest of many big problems which arise in relation to a second front is the problem of shipping. When you remember how many hundreds and hundreds of vessels were required for the evacuation of a relatively small army from Dunkirk without equipment, you may well imagine how staggering would be the force of ships, both civil and military, needed for the transport of a large army with equipment to a hostile coast.

Then consider the Middle East. Every now and then we read of some gallant and battered convoy, with half its ships gone, arriving at Malta or Alexandria. We may also think of the score of ships that must round the Cape to go into the Middle East by the back door.

The shipping strain is tremendous. It must all be accepted for the maintenance of a military position which is of far-reaching importance. And yet we are occupying on the western approach to Egypt only a very small German force, merely a trifling fraction of the great German force which is being occupied on the Russian frontier.

And the Far East. The problem of American aid to Australia is mostly a problem of shipping. Our own transport problems in Australia are largely those of shipping.

So that, wherever we look, shipping is the great problem.

When I was in England last year, the democratic world was losing far more ships than it was building. It is indeed comforting to know that to-day the United States and Great Britain are somewhat more than overtaking their losses. But we cannot be saved merely by holding our own. The construction, equipping and manning of ships must go on to a point where overwhelming carrying and fighting capacity on the water is developed.

That the United Nations will out-produce the Axis Powers in aircraft and guns and tanks and bombs I do not doubt. The almost incredible industrial resources of the United States alone would guarantee this. But the grim truth remains that you win wars in the long run by bringing superior forces and equipment to the point of battle. Fifty thousand tanks in the United States will not defeat Germany so surely as will five thousand shipped to and actually engaged in Europe. We read of enormous aircraft production in the United States. The output of a week or two shipped to this theatre would give to Australia an impregnable strength to resist Japanese attack.

Any conception of this war is inadequate which envisages a state of affairs in which each Allied country is so furnished with men and equipment that it cannot successfully be attacked, but in which each of them is also without that overwhelming equipment for the sea which will enable it to move to the offensive.

It is elementary sense that we cannot begin to win the war —and we have certainly not begun to win it yet—without getting on to the offensive. But to talk of the offensive is mere meaningless chatter unless we have the vital means for conducting the attack. And in this world, with its map reshaped as it has been in the last three years, the essential for the attack is power on the sea.

And so I come back to the conclusion that, once more, the winning of a great war for survival is inextricably bound up with naval power, and with the skill, tenacity and courage of those who "go down to the sea in ships".

18 September, 1942.

XXIX

THE STATUTE OF WESTMINSTER

This week we have had a very interesting debate at Canberra about the adoption of certain sections of the Statute of Westminster, which was passed through the British Parliament in 1931, but certain detailed provisions of which do not apply to Australia unless adopted by the Australian Parliament.

The problems involved are the subject of a good deal of misunderstanding, and a few minutes devoted to their explanation may therefore be useful.

Even before the last war the story of the growth of the British Empire from Great Britain itself to its colonies, with those colonies subsequently becoming self-governing colonies, and then self-governing dominions, made up the most fascinating example of constitutional growth in the history of the world.

Long before the last war, self-government in the dominions had been fully recognized by the mother country. Theoretically, the British Parliament could pass laws for any dominion, but in practice there was no possibility of this being done except at the request of the dominion.

During and shortly after the last war, however, there was an acute development in the theory of Empire relations. This development was to a large extent the result of pressure from such dominions as Canada and South Africa, each of which had its own local racial problem and each of which, for various reasons, was more disposed to require a written definition of its position than were either ourselves or the New Zealanders.

L

In the upshot, in 1926, at the Imperial Conference of that year—at which we were represented by Mr Bruce—the whole problem was discussed and a formula set out in what is now called the Balfour Declaration, the best-known passage in which is that describing the status of the United Kingdom and her dominions:

They are autonomous communities within the British Empire, equal in status, in no way subordinate one to another in any aspect of their domestic or external affairs though united by a common allegi· ance to the Crown and freely associated as members of the British Commonwealth of Nations.

Subsequently a committee was set up to conduct certain technical examinations into some of the legal results of this declaration. That committee reported to the Imperial Conference of 1930, which recommended that a declaratory act of Parliament on the whole subject should be passed by the Parliament of the United Kingdom.

What subsequently became the Statute of Westminster was then drafted, but it was agreed that it should not be introduced into the Parliament at Westminster until it had been requested and consented to by the various dominion parliaments. The necessary resolutions were in fact submitted to the Common-wealth Parliament in 1931, being carried by both Houses, and the Statute of Westminster was then, at the end of 1931, enacted.

Five sections of the Act, dealing with such matters as the power of the Commonwealth Parliament to pass laws incon-sistent with British statutes—provided of course that they are otherwise within the power of the Australian Parliament—and the right of the Commonwealth Parliament to give extra-terri-torial effect to its laws, were not to operate in Australia, New Zealand or Newfoundland unless adopted by the parliament of any such dominion.

Now, a great many people appear to think that adopting these relatively minor provisions in some way affects the status of Australia and its relation to the other countries of the British Empire, and in particular to Great Britain.

This is not so. Those portions of the Statute of Westminster which concern themselves with the status of the dominions became law at the end of 1931, and needed no adoption by Australia beyond the resolutions which were carried eleven years ago.

The preamble to the Statute of Westminster, which has a declaratory character, is already law. It became law eleven years ago, and nothing we can think or say or do now can affect it.

It establishes in terms the proposition that "The Crown is the symbol of the free association of the members of the British Commonwealth of Nations", and that "They are united by a common allegiance to the Crown". These, following upon the Balfour Declaration of 1926, are the words which deal with the relations of the countries of the British Empire. They were not up for consideration this week because—and I want to emphasize this point—they were passed eleven years ago at the request of all the dominions, and whether we like it or not they operate to-day.

I may say at once that I have two great quarrels with the language that was used. In the first place, I think that to endeavour to put into written form a relation part of whose strength rested upon its very vagueness and want of definition, was a cardinal blunder. There was a living spirit, and we endeavoured to imprison it within the four corners of a legal formula. My second criticism is that the legal formula was itself so ambiguous that it has ever since given rise to disputes of interpretation, and may give rise to even more serious ones in the years to come.

A good illustration of this is to be found in the quite honest difference of opinion which exists as to the way in which Australia makes war. The Attorney-General in the present Government went to great pains, when Japan came into the war, to follow a procedure which would indicate that His Majesty the King was declaring war on Japan in respect of Australia on the advice of his Australian ministers. This seems to me to be based upon the view that, though the King makes peace and makes war, he could be at war with Japan in relation to Great Britain and at the same time, if his Australian ministers had happened so to advise, he could be at peace with Japan in relation to Australia, just as he is, on the same theory, at peace with Germany in relation to Southern Ireland.

Quite candidly, this theory is beyond me. I do not understand how one king can be at peace and at war at the same time in relation to the same foreign power, unless we, so to speak, carve him up into six kings: the King of England, the King of South Africa, the King of Australia, and so on—a notion which was strongly maintained by General Hertzog in some conversations I had with him in 1935. But it seems to me to be a complete denial of the proposition that the Crown is the symbol of association, or that we have a common allegiance to the Throne. Quite frankly, I do not accept the theory that a dominion can be a neutral in a British war and at the same time remain within the British Empire.

Neutrality means secession. If this were not so, then the association between the various portions of the Empire, imposing no liabilities, would be no more than a friendly gesture, and would certainly stop far short of being even an ordinary military alliance.

I cannot, in the time open to me, elaborate this, but I hope that I have sufficiently conveyed to you what I have in mind.

But all these questions, which concern themselves with vital matters, turn upon what was done in 1926 and in 1930-31, and are in no way affected by the relatively minor technical questions that we have just been considering at Canberra.

Thus it is that, although I have, as you will have gathered, the strongest views on the question of Empire relations, I can see no reason at all why an otherwise perfectly valid Australian law should become invalid because somebody manages to dig up an old English statute which is inconsistent with it. Nor can I see why the power of this country to make laws having extra-territorial operation should not be put beyond doubt. Why, the whole possibility of enforcing conscription may depend upon it. Nor can I see why doubts about such matters as the validity of our shipping laws and of our Admiralty jurisdiction should not be resolved.

These are all relatively minor matters. They are, as one might say, the mere incidentals of the great decisions which were taken years ago.

We in the parliamentary Opposition thought that, having regard to the misunderstandings which do arise on this question, it would have been wise to impose some delay upon the passing of the Adoption Bill, but the Government did not agree.

The whole purpose of this broadcast has been to endeavour to put the matter in its right perspective. It is essentially a Bill of relatively minor importance. It derives its chief interest from the fact that it refers us back to the controversies of 1931 and reminds us, if we are given to thinking about such problems, that in our Empire relations we have by no means reached either finality or certainty.

9 October, 1942.

XXX

SCHOOLS AND THE WAR

DEMANDS for man power and woman power in the war are increasing and pressing. They represent a problem on which the Government must be the ultimate judge and which must cause any Government the greatest anxiety. Such demands are in any circumstances hard to criticize or to resist, for the safety of the people is the supreme law, and nobody is in so good a position to estimate what safety requires as the Government of the country.

But demands should always be related to supply and to real needs. So far as we can we must have in mind, even while the war is raging, the essential non-military needs of the nation, including those things that we must have if we are successfully to encounter the vast, complex and menacing problems of the peace which is to come.

One of the most important of these things, easily overlooked at a time like this, is an educated community. We of our generation have been neither particularly clever nor particularly wise, for our record is strewn with want of foresight, want of preparation, selfishness, lack of understanding of the economic forces which can play so much havoc in the world, want of recognition of those greater moral forces which mould the relation of man to man.

And so war has come with its crises, its grim dangers, its dreadful price exacted for past neglects, its false material prosperity masking the fact that savings, accumulated resources, are being eaten up, and that immense problems of rebuilding are round the corner.

Do you ever, even in a fleeting moment, think of the enormous questions which will confront both us and the world when the war is over—questions international, economic and moral? I am sure you do. I do, and with some apprehension. For I doubt whether they can be solved either sensibly or safely unless we are much better and more intelligent people after the war than we were before it. Above all, we shall need clear minds, honest minds, courageous minds, well-informed minds; in a word, educated minds. For the simple and unpalatable truth is that our democratic system cannot continue if its motive power is to be a mixture of class selfishness, materialism, disregard of minorities, and a somewhat lazy indifference to the future.

Apart from the winning of the war, the greatest because the most fundamental task in front of us is to educate a new generation, not for mere money-making or to comply with the law, but for an enlightened citizenship based upon honest thinking and human understanding.

That brings me to the position of the schools. They are even at this moment, and in the jargon of the moment, an "essential industry". It is their great privilege and sublime duty to prepare the minds of the post-war adult generation—the real founders of the post-war order—the generation which will either build a lasting and a just peace or go lightly and blindly down "the primrose path which leads to the everlasting bonfire". So often the present seems to us the absorbing problem. We live in it. We often hate to look beyond it. But over the entrance to every school might well be written in letters of gold the words, "Here we deal with the future". And so it is that the present position of our schools is important. I believe that we should endeavour to do to the best of our capacity at least two things:

First, we should as far as possible retain the services of our teachers, both male and female. Some schools in Australia are, I believe, suffering greatly from a drain upon their teaching staffs. These include many girls' schools, where natural and patriotic instincts take younger teachers away from their school-teaching and into work which has, to them, a more obvious war significance and value. One of my purposes to-night is to endeavour to make it clear that the training of the new generation is war work and peace work of the supremest importance.

Second, we should do our best to preserve the concentration of schoolboys and schoolgirls on those matters which relate to their training and education. The post-war problems are, to my mind, so enormous and their solution will call for a so much higher standard of public intelligence than we have been prone to exhibit in the past that it is essential that the generation now coming into flower should be a sound and competent and well-balanced one, and not a war-racked, nervy and uneducated one. This would be singularly like a counsel of perfection in a country subject to almost daily bombing, but in Australia we are so fortunately placed that we should well decide that the younger children of our nation are to suffer as little of the impairment of war as determination on our part can ensure.

I hope you will not think me merely peevish if I say that in the past, in public affairs, too many of us have distrusted the educated mind. Indeed, I think it would be not inaccurate to say that on the whole we have given inadequate recognition to the expert, trained mind. I was forcibly struck recently, when reading the estimates at Canberra, by the fact that in one scientific department we pay highly trained scientific research workers with university degrees only £4 a week more than we pay to the labourers about the premises. I am the last to underrate the man who has, in a phrase once heard in the Federal Parliament, "graduated with honours in the University of Life". I know that it may be no particular credit to a man to be the holder of a university degree, which in any event may be no more than a licence to practise some special profession for a good fee. But, other things being equal, the educated mind should be more apt to be detached and balanced; to see both sides of a question; to understand the opponent. It should be more apt to take the long view, which is so commonly right, and disregard the short view, which is so commonly wrong.

Our ablest men must be attracted to political service, not the most fluent or the best-advertised. To the civil service must go more and more of the products of universities. Into the world of business must go better and better educated recruits, so that business may learn that there is a second profit and loss account which collates the credit and debit entries of the particular business in relation to its industrial and social obligations. Higher education for women must come to be regarded as normal, and not as the eccentricity of a potential "blue stocking". For the blunt fact is that the equality of the sexes cannot be maintained if a slapdash training in a few minor ornamental accomplishments is considered an adequate education for the daughter of the house.

And so I come back to the basic truth of this matter, which is that we must constantly look forward. The generation which is now in charge was at school just before or during the last war. The German schools, more than anything else, produced this Nazi generation which has blazed its trail of savagery across Europe.

What will our schools produce? On the answer to that question will depend the future of Australia.

16 October, 1942.

XXXI

THE MORAL ELEMENT IN TOTAL WAR

THE obvious aspects of a war effort are material. We must raise and equip armed forces, mine coal and ore, manufacture iron and steel, make munitions, supply and maintain transport, produce and distribute foodstuffs, build ships, in brief, do a thousand and one things which involve man power and material power and money power.

During the last three years we have in Australia done an immense work on all those matters with inevitably increasing momentum. And the doing of them has had many incidental consequences. There is more money in circulation. There is tremendous taxation but, at the same time, a good deal of new material prosperity.

In order partially to counteract these things we have had some necessary rationing of certain essentials, though we have permitted ourselves a good deal of extravagance on non-essentials.

(Incidentally, these material factors have aggravated, if they have not actually created, such problems as those of the abuse of liquor, because relatively easy money in many hands is not always wisely or soberly spent.)

But I am referring to these material factors not to disparage or underestimate their importance, but to try to put them in their proper proportion.

A total war effort requires not only that the body shall fight or work, but also that the mind and spirit shall fight and work. Our factory production may have reached enormous heights, but he would be indeed a comfortable man who did not find all about him far too much inequality of sacrifice, indifference, slackness, unawareness of danger or of urgency, and rampant selfishness.

Whatever the efforts of any Government or group of industrial leaders, there can be no complete national organization of men and materials and financial resources unless there is ever present and ever active a vital moral element in the community which produces an utter willingness to share in sacrifice and effort. This fundamental moral problem is not one about which any of us need be unduly pious or self-righteous. A fair and square consideration of it calls us to a ruthless self-examination. It demands that there should be uncommonly frank answers to uncommonly blunt questions.

It is no part of my function or yours to give credit to all the rumours or complaints which come constantly to our ears, but if a fraction of them is true, there is need for some pretty plain interrogations. Let me put a few to you.

Are there any or many cases of employers on cost-plus-profit defence contracts who are willing to build up overtime and costs in order to increase the profit? Are there any or many cases of employees going slowly on ordinary work in order to build up more overtime at loaded rates of pay? Are there any or many who are doing well out of the war and not saving for the future, but leaving it to the Government to attend to their troubles when the war is over? Are there thousands whose motto is, "Let us eat, drink and be merry, for to-morrow somebody else will die"? Are there thousands of us who have no conception of discipline as self-discipline, but who respond only to some authority from outside ourselves?

The problem around which such questions as these centre is really desperately important, but there can be no passionate patriotism or willing self-sacrifice in war unless we know in our hearts that we are fighting for good things against evil things, and there can be no better world order except on a moral basis. The brain of man may devise wonders and the hand of man execute them, but they will all fall into evil and harmful uses unless the heart of man—the guide of conduct—is sound and true. This is true whatever systems we may choose for the accomplishment of our ends.

Capitalism cannot rebuild the world aright except on a basis of humane and enlightened responsibility to the community. Socialism, if it merely means provision of bread and circuses for all by a supposedly inexhaustible State, must fail calamitously. The real essence of a true socialist movement must be a quite revolutionary spiritual sense of the overwhelming obligation of man to his neighbour.

True, the Russian communist revolution was avowedly based upon the purely materialist conceptions of Karl Marx; but if there is one thing which stands out in the recent history of Russia, it is that the Russian people have developed on top of the Marxian doctrines a burning spirit of faith and determination as far removed from materialism as the earth is from the sun.

Indeed, as you look around the world in this war you cannot fail to be struck by the fact that the successes have so far gone to the nations which have a faith, even though a false one. We may and do violently disagree with the object of the beliefs of Germans or Japanese, but it would be a foolish observer who did not concede that the resurgence of Germany as a terrific military power is largely to be attributed to Hitler's youth movement, and to the burning belief that it acquired and preached in its leader, its nation and its destiny.

The question we need to put to ourselves most frequently in

these days is, "What do we believe in?" If our clever and cynical attitude is to be that we believe in nothing, then that is what we are likely to be left with at the finish. If our answer is to be that we believe in pounds, shillings and pence, bricks and mortar and nothing else, I am at a loss to understand why we should really claim to be entitled, almost as of right, to victory. It is only a faith in something that goes beyond these purely physical matters which can really inspire a nation to honest self-sacrifice and carry its armies to that ultimate victory which we believe truth must always have over falsehood.

In most things in this war we must press on, we must go forward, we must neither look back nor go back. But in one thing I believe that we must go back. We must, before this struggle even begins to end, go back to the simple virtues and to the simple ways of life.

If war to us is an interruption, unavoidable but irritating, something cut out of our normal living and not something dynamic put into it, then our attitude towards its problems will inevitably be to give as little as possible and to get as much. We shall be unmoved by the spectacle of unlimited sacrifice on the field of battle and bigger and better bonuses and rewards on the home front. We shall continue to save for the Government's tremendous financial problem at a rate which is, in plain terms, a national disgrace. That a whole year of unexampled employment and wages in a country itself untouched by war should produce a beggarly £9,000,000 worth of war savings certificates is bitter evidence of a wrong moral approach to the war.

If this war were to us not an irritating interruption but the supreme challenge; the most crowded, moving and stimulating period through which we shall have lived; a period when we are the responsible trustees for the future happiness and just living of all people, things would be changed in a flash. No longer would the question be, "How much can I get?" or "How little can I do?" but, "What can I give?" or, in the immortal words, " 'What can I do to be saved?' "

That most Australians understand this, I cannot doubt. But that too many of us are blind to it is a melancholy proof that the moral element in total war has yet to assume its full significance in our national effort.

21 August, 1942.

XXXII

THE LAW AND THE CITIZEN

BECAUSE certain States have decided to exercise their rights to test the validity of the new taxation laws under which the Commonwealth is to impose income tax for both Commonwealth and State purposes, their Premiers are being accused in some quarters of improper conduct.

The testing of the constitutional validity of a far-reaching law is described by one journal as "forensic hair-splitting". A spate of criticism gushes out, all based on the idea that to uphold the Constitution in time of war is undesirable, even if it is not actually subversive. I say "to uphold the Constitution" because, if the High Court finds the laws valid, the Constitution will be upheld and the Commonwealth's power to make these laws judicially affirmed, while, if it finds the laws invalid, it will be because the upholding of the Constitution requires that result. The appeal to the Court is therefore simply the appeal to the Constitution, whose interpreter the Court is.

Now, why is this thought to be improper? There is here such confusion of thought that I want, as a lawyer of experience and a responsible and sober public man, to discuss it with you.

My own proposition is this: that this war is one for law and order, in other words for international security under international law. It is a war for freedom; and that hackneyed phrase, if we understand it, means that we are fighting to preserve that equal justice under the law which it has taken centuries of our history, and much blood and sacrifice, to produce. It is a queer notion that justice according to law, should be accounted nothing —or even "forensic hair-splitting"—when our very freedom depends upon it.

At this moment our men are fighting for our hearths and homes. Yes, but also for a free Parliament, for open and incorruptible courts of justice, for the even administration of laws freely enacted and honourably obeyed.

If we think with horror and repugnance of Nazi tyranny it is because, under the brutish practices of the Putsch and the Gestapo, the law is no man's protector, and the judges, ceasing to be his defenders, become the agents of oppression.

Do not let us begin to think lightly of the law. Its rule, its power, its authority, are at the centre of our civilization.

The great advocate, Erskine, speaking in court in 1792, said, "If I were to ask you, gentlemen of the jury, what is the choicest fruit that grows upon the tree of English liberty, you would answer 'Security under the law'. If I were to ask the whole people of England the return they looked for at the hands of government for the burdens under which they bend to support it, I should still be answered 'Security under the law'." Those words are as true to-day as when they were spoken, and they were spoken in a year when revolution was running red riot in France; when England, led by the younger Pitt, was within a few months of war with France—with a Napoleon ready within two years to win his first victory against the English, and to begin his fluttering and threatening of the entire civilized world.

Of all laws, that of the Constitution is at once the most fundamental and the most sacred. Parliaments may tell us from day to day what we are to do or not to do. The Parliaments themselves are controlled by the Constitution, which is not their servant but, on the contrary, their master.

The Commonwealth Constitution is the organic law under which the Commonwealth Parliament and the Commonwealth Government are set up and exercise their functions.

Neither Parliament nor Government can alter it. Only the people can do that. They were its creators forty years ago. They are its masters still.

You will at once see, if you have followed me so far, that to ignore the Constitution, to treat its structure and the limitations it imposes upon the powers of the Commonwealth Parliament as of no account, to endeavour by clamour to prevent recourse to the courts for its interpretation, is to violate the whole conception of the rule of law. It is to the credit of the Commonwealth Government that its responsible spokesmen have taken no part in this clamour.

If inciting people to disregard and disobey some petty local statute is an offence, is it to be a sign of merit to incite them to disregard and disobey the basic law under which our free institutions live?

These things have only to be thought about to be clearly understood.

If the day is to come when the courts are to be closed to the aggrieved citizen, when the King's writ is not to run because popular uproar wills it so, when the appeal to the law is to be an occasion of scoffing, then that day will cast a black shadow across British freedom. For Erskine's "security under the law", mark you, is not such security as your opponents, being in a majority, may concede; it is not something precariously dependent upon the whim of a mob. It is that security to which a man may confidently and calmly appeal, even though every man's hand may be against him. The law's greatest benefits are for the minority man—the individual.

M

Whatever public opinion may be—and most of us know little of the merits of this taxation argument, and will know but little more until our assessments come in—the Premiers have a perfect right, and indeed a duty, to see that whatever is done by any Parliament of this country is done in accordance with the powers conferred upon it by the supreme law of the land.

12 June, 1942.

XXXIII

THE NATURE OF DEMOCRACY

WE human beings are easily enslaved by language. A few words suitably grouped into a slogan or catch-cry may acquire such a flashy attractiveness that they are easily mistaken for an entire philosophy. To be a maker of good phrases is to travel half the journey towards popular power.

The curious thing is that, as time goes on and unthinking acceptance of some cant phrase settles into a fixed habit of mind, some words acquire a sacrosanct character, whilst others lose their original meaning and fall into abuse and decay.

Perhaps the best example of a word which has become almost sacrosanct is the word "democracy". We see in it the symbol of our liberties. We see it as the enemy of Nazi and Fascist tyrannies. We attach to it a sort of universal quality of truth. In a country like our own, you may no more pronounce yourself not a democrat than you may avow yourself a house-breaker. We disagree among ourselves on almost every conceivable subject, but we are all democrats.

This general and tacit acceptance of democracy is paradoxically not only a source of strength but also one of our greatest dangers. For a faith which rests not upon experience or understanding but upon a mere ritual, is so much the husk of a belief that it can be winnowed away by the first high wind. We must understand and experience democracy if democracy is to be a living faith and is to survive.

With your permission, and I hope encouragement, I propose

to occupy a few of my sessions in an examination of democracy —its true nature, its past faults, its vital significance and function in the rebuilding of the world after the war. It will be my theme that we have misunderstood, ignored and occasionally despised democracy, and that if in the new political generation we practise democracy as badly as we did in the past, either democracy will disappear or the rebuilt world will be foundationless and will fall.

First, then, what is democracy? No well-worn epigram will answer this question. In its strict etymological sense it means government by the people, that is popular self-government as opposed to autocracy or aristocracy, or any other system which separates the rulers from the ruled. In another sense it connotes an attitude of mind—a civic sense of men's equality in the eye of the State. In its narrowest and most colloquial sense it comes down to an election cry or two—"One man one vote", "One vote one value". Some people see in it an almost divine character: to them the voice of the people is the voice of God. At least one Greek thinker dismissed it with the contemptuous observation that under it the votes of the many would be used to steal the property of the few.

In my own opinion, our most grievous error has been that we have thought too much of democracy in mechanical terms— as a system of government—and too little of it as a spirit, a moving force; not a mere vehicle for the expression of the human mind alone, but a challenge to the human spirit.

In our country, democracy expresses itself, mechanically speaking, in a parliamentary system which gives to every adult citizen of both sexes, every three years or so, a vote in the election of a member of Parliament who will help to make laws, and through him a voice in the selection of a cabinet of ministers who will administer those laws.

That system was the outcome of centuries of struggle and evolution. It was finally achieved quite recently—in my own lifetime—when women got the vote. The instrument of popular self-government was then complete. But—and I emphasize the "but"—democracy's task did not then end; it began.

It is a good thing to win a historic struggle for freedom. It is a better thing still to know how to use your freedom when you have won it. I may have the most expensive and perfect piano in the world, but it will give out only crashing discords unless I learn to play it. And when I have learnt the mere mechanics of playing it, my knowledge will be no more than a curse to my neighbours and my friends unless I catch something of the spirit of music, and learn that subtle magic which converts ordered noise into celestial harmony.

No, democracy is more than a piece of equipment. The fact that, for a score of years we have—the privilege of self-government attained—delegated its exercise to a relatively few patriotic and earnest, or ambitious and noisy, people, asking for ourselves only that we shall be left alone to our money-making or our pleasures, is the best proof that we have attached no value to a system the essence of which we have not tried to understand.

I repeat, the problem of democracy began when democracy was achieved. If government were by a despot, amiable or vicious, we, as the governed, might well shrug our shoulders and resign ourselves to fate. But when government of ourselves is by ourselves, we must bestir ourselves. If, then, there is tyranny, it is our own. If there is injustice, we have ordered or permitted it. If there is hunger or unemployment, we must look to ourselves for the remedy. For when we are the masters as well as the servants, we cannot either wisely or usefully blame others for bad direction or faulty planning or fumbling execution. To stand erect and say, "I am one of the rulers of my country"—there is a position of dignity and of responsibility. Yet, they are a dignity and a responsibility which democracy, properly understood, gives to every grown man and woman in this nation.

But a true conception of democracy goes even beyond this, for democracy is more than a machine; it is a spirit. It is based upon the Christian conception that there is in every human soul a spark of the divine; that, with all their inequalities of mind and body, the souls of men stand equal in the sight of God. So it is that, while Fascists and Nazis concentrate their efforts upon the power of the State, regarding the citizen as the mere minister to that power, democrats must concern themselves with what they see to be the true end and final justification of the State—a full and good life for every individual citizen. The chief end of man ceases to be the upholding of the power of the State; the chief end of the State becomes man—man the individual, man the immortal spirit.

Once we see this, we begin to see all. Democracy is viewed, not just as one more system of government, appearing and disappearing in the march of history, but as a spirit which adjusts man to man, which lends dignity to labour, which moves constantly towards the light.

Now, if this spirit is of the essence of democracy, can we rightly say that we have understood or practised it. For, if man is to be adjusted to man, if we are to live together in mutual amity and justice, if we are to be dignified without being proud or overbearing, we must be givers rather than receivers; we must be quick to discharge our duties and modest about our rights. For the harmony and brotherly love of a family is not maintained on a basis of claims. In the wise language of the Bible, the family are "in honour preferring one another".

When we go to the polling booths, do we really go hoping,

by our vote, to prefer the interests of others to our own? This is not an unreal question. I am not asking for or expecting a community of archangels or of martyrs. I am not asking for an orgy of self-destruction. There is no necessary antithesis between our own interests and desires and the good of our neighbour. But if, as a voter, I am concerned only with my own advantage and am indifferent to the cost to others, I am simply corrupt. I am selling my vote for an individual mess of pottage. Government of the people by my party, for me, is not democracy. It is just a system of crooked bargaining. It cannot support any decent new order, and it is not worth fighting for.

So, our first task as professing democrats is to examine both our faith and ourselves. We must no longer fob ourselves off with loose thinking and windy words. To some of us, democracy has meant a sort of false back-slapping good-fellowship, with Jack and his master rollicking together; to some of us, democracy has meant an open-handedness with other people's money; to others, a cynical sort of system under which it is better to be foolish and win than to be wise and suffer defeat. But it is only that democracy which sees the superb spiritual value of the individual man which can really win a crusade against tyranny and force, and lead the way into a better world.

23 October, 1942.

XXXIV

THE SICKNESS OF DEMOCRACY

Last week I spoke to you about the nature of democracy. I am sure you will agree that it is a problem worth the best thought we can put into it. To-night I want to say something to you about the sickness from which democracy has suffered. This is important, for if we are unwilling to study the course of the disease we shall be quite unfit to discover the cure.

For a generation now, in Australia and elsewhere, we have not been doing our best with democracy. On the contrary, we have frequently done our worst. This statement can, I imagine, be readily proved if we consider our political history during that period.

Parliament should, if popular self-government is to be good government—indeed the best government—represent the cream of the nation. For, if we value and understand the privilege of choosing our own rulers from among ourselves, how strange that we should not be at pains to find and appoint our wisest and our best citizens! If we are shareholders or directors seeking a manager, with what closeness shall we scrutinize the applicant and consider his abilities and record! But to the abilities and record of those who are to manage the affairs of the nation we have, all too frequently, been sublimely indifferent.

I went into politics for the first time fourteen years ago. Many of my friends shrugged their shoulders at what they obviously thought a harmless eccentricity. The most generous unspoken comment was, "Another good man gone wrong!" It was plainly not thought by many that the government of the country was as important as the practice of the law.

During those fourteen years I have, times without number, heard the loud complaint of the business man about the politician. I have, as you have, repeatedly heard the statement that "What the country needs is a Government of business men." On scores of occasions I have made the obvious rejoinder, "All right, what's preventing you? Why not go into Parliament yourself?" And then, as in the old story, "they all, with one accord, began to make excuse." One was too busy—as if only the leisured or the unemployed were needed in Parliament. One would lose too much money—as if serving the people in Parliament ought to be a profitable job. One could not face the bitter criticism and misrepresentation through which the parliamentary candidate so often has to wade—as if only the thick-skinned are fit to devise the laws of the land. And so on. All excuses, masking the fundamental fact that the business of politics was disregarded as fit only for loud-mouthed careerists. It was, and is, very depressing. What should be, if we understood democracy, the noblest and highest of civil vocations, degraded into something of less importance than the higgling of the market and the acquisition of wealth!

Now, what has been the effect of this on Parliament itself? Surely it has been to make it very little more than an average representation of the people. It is, in my experience, a perfect cross-section: all sorts of occupations, all sorts of men, almost always possessed—contrary to cheap rumour—of honesty and decency, and anxiety to do the right thing. As a jury of the nation, it would be hard to improve it. But the world's progress depends in the first instance not on the average man, but on what Confucius called the "superior man". The great movements of history have sprung from a few uncommon men. Great rulers, Prime Ministers, Presidents, ministers of State, must be men who are above the ordinary. A great democratic Parliament must provide the leaders of the people, not merely an average reflection of a fleeting popular will.

I hope nobody is so foolish as to think that the problems in front of us in the next ten years can be solved without hard thinking and infinite labour, not by a jury of men in the street but by the very best brains and courage that this country can select.

Again, we have been at fault in our failure to maintain a constant and steady interest in the government of the country. If we come to life only at election times and go back to in-difference or grumbling criticism for the years that intervene, our political judgment, being based on no continuing principle, will be spasmodic, uncertain and inconsistent. We shall take only short views, and the candidate who plays up to them will be elected. Yet, a moment's reflection should tell us that only long-range thinking and planning can save either democracy or the world.

It was taking the long view which restored Russia. It was living from day to day in a jumble of short-sighted politics which cast down France. Can we expect long-range thinking from a Parliament which we have all too frequently chosen for its capacity to cater for our short-range selfishness?

To all this sickness of democracy, the Press has, I fear, made its contribution. We are all influenced by what we read, and particularly by what we read in the news columns. The parlia-mentary items will quickly colour our outlook upon Parliament and the nature of our interest in its debates and doings. Yet for many years every new member of Parliament has been quickly taught that a much speedier entrance into the headlines is guaranteed by a five minutes' exchange of personalities on the floor of the House than by an hour's thoughtful contribution on a problem of great moment.

This has been a real tragedy, for it has induced a good deal of contempt for Parliament, and it has given to the word "politician" a connotation and a flavour—a sort of sneering quality—which is not only grossly unjust to the many men who give honourable service in public places, but is infinitely damaging to representative government.

This misconception has extended to the civil service—that indispensable instrument of government, democratic or otherwise. Do not underrate the civil servant. He is for the most part anonymous and unadvertised, but he is responsible for by far the greater part of the achievements sometimes loudly claimed by others. He provides, as a witty friend of mine once said, "a level of competence below which no Government can fall". He has done a marvellous job in this war. His importance will grow, not diminish, for Government activity is here to stay.

Obviously, then, we should be at pains to look to the future, and recruit the very best young men and women for the civil service. Yet most of our great public schools have for many years neglected this fact, considering the professions more important, while a move some years back to provide for the entrance of a certain number of university graduates into the Commonwealth public service each year was resisted by many members on the astonishing ground that the move was "undemocratic". Does democracy demand that managing directors should be recruited only from office boys? Is not democracy entitled to the best minds and the best training in those who are to serve it?

These cheap fallacies and superstitions, which appear to include a belief that it is undemocratic to be educated, will destroy us unless we destroy them.

Next, we have increasingly misunderstood and debased the function of the member of Parliament. We have treated him as a paid delegate to run our errands and obey our wishes, and not as a representative, bound, as Edmund Burke so nobly said, to bring his "matured judgment" to the service of his electors. We encourage our members of Parliament to tremble at the thought of a hostile public meeting, and expect them to flutter in the breeze caused by thousands of printed forms demanding this or that, and signed with suitable threats by carefully canvassed voters.

Quite bluntly, if you want paid agents, hired men, bound to do your bidding even when they know or believe that you are wrong, anxious at all costs to keep your favour, their eyes turned always towards the next election, then you will get a Parliament of the spineless, and democracy will disappear. For political systems have much more frequently been overthrown by their own corruption and decay than by external forces.

My own father, who was and is a good democrat, and was for some years a member of the Victorian Parliament, had the excellent habit, whenever he heard that his electors were disagreeing with some vote of his in the House, of going straight away to visit them and addressing a meeting to explain why he thought he was right and the meeting was wrong. His simple and accurate belief was that the first function of a member of Parliament was to be a man and not a phonograph record, a guide and not a mere follower.

Finally, and most importantly, we have not succeeded in elevating democracy into a living faith. We have become sceptical and indifferent. Freedom has for too many become a word and not a passion. I sometimes wonder whether freedom in any of its shapes is clearly seen by us as the living element in our history and the principal object of the democratic system.

The best epitaph for a true democrat will not be, "I tickled people's ears, I got their votes, I spent their money", but, "I have fought a good fight, I have finished my course, I have kept the faith."

There can be no doubt that this democracy of ours has been very sick. If and when it can be cured, it has great work to do. But it will never be cured unless we see the past clearly, and recognize frankly that we cannot ignore politics and treat democracy as a mere matter of loaves and fishes and demean the politician, and at the same time sensibly demand that "government of the people by the people and for the people shall not perish from the earth".

30 October, 1942.

XXXV

THE ACHIEVEMENTS OF DEMOCRACY

I HAVE endeavoured briefly to look at the true nature of democracy, and to diagnose its modern illness. Let me to-night say something of its achievements, for the justification of democracy is not theoretical but is woven into the practical fabric of history.

It is easy to criticize the philosophic basis of democracy, to say that to decide wisdom by merely counting heads is absurd, to dilate upon the alleged inefficiency of democracy and to contrast it with the alleged efficiency of dictatorships. There is an old Latin tag which reminds us that there is a temptation to regard as magnificent everything which is unknown. We have been too close to democracy to appreciate it. But it is not easy to ignore its achievements. Let me speak to you of them to-night.

Democracy has proved itself a friend of peace. No fully self-governing country has provoked a war within a century's memory. Autocracy, Fascism, Nazism—these so naturally express themselves in terms of power that they have by nature become aggressive. This is inevitable, for the motive of power, once ingrained in a people, leads easily to a feeling that conquest is the law of life. No aggression by any democracy led to the present war. Designs upon Czechoslovakia, Poland, Norway, Denmark, Belgium, Holland, were German, not British or French.

There is a good reason for this. Democracy, being founded upon the rights of the individual citizens, concerns itself first and foremost with the domestic well-being of its people. It occupies itself with political and social and industrial reform. The very reason why it begins war "behind scratch" is that it has preferred preparations and expenditure for peace to the provision of great armaments. In the grim struggle between guns and butter, it prefers butter. It feels in its bones that war is a destroyer, and that conqueror and conquered may be at the end "in one red burial blent".

When, in the Atlantic Charter, the Prime Minister of the United Kingdom and the President of the United States of America declared their common principles, it was fitting that the first principle should be that "These countries seek no aggrandisement, territorial or otherwise." The fundamental democratic principle is one of peace and international goodwill.

The concentration of democracy upon the welfare of the citizen has in the last century produced great and indeed astonishing results. In a famous chapter of his *History of England*, written a hundred years ago, Macaulay spoke of the "good old days". He said:

It is natural that, being dissatisfied with the present, we should form a too favourable estimate of the past.

In truth we are under a deception similar to that which misleads the traveller in the Arabian desert. Beneath the caravan all is dry and bare; but far in advance, and far in the rear, is the semblance of refreshing waters. The pilgrims hasten forward and find nothing but sand where, an hour before, they had seen a lake. They turn their eyes and see a lake where, an hour before, they were toiling through sand. A similar illusion seems to haunt nations through every stage of the long progress from poverty and barbarism to the highest degrees of opulence and civilization. But, if we resolutely chase the mirage backward, we shall find it recede before us into the regions of fabulous antiquity. It is now the fashion to place the golden age of England in times when noblemen were destitute of comforts the want of which would be intolerable to a modern footman, when farmers and shopkeepers breakfasted on loaves the very sight of which would raise a riot in a modern workhouse, when to have a clean shirt once a week was a privilege reserved for the higher class of gentry, when men died faster in the purest country air than they now die in the most pestilential lanes of our towns, and when men died faster in the lanes of our towns than they now die on the coast of Guiana. We too shall, in our turn, be outstripped, and in our turn be envied. It may well be, in the twentieth century, that the peasant of Dorsetshire may think himself miserably paid with twenty shillings a week; that the carpenter at Greenwich may receive ten shillings a day; that labouring men may be as little used to dine without meat as they now are to eat rye bread; that sanitary police and medical discoveries may have added several more years to the average length of human life; that numerous comforts and luxuries which are now unknown, or confined to a few, may be within the reach of every diligent and thrifty working man. And yet it may then be the mode to assert that the increase of wealth and the progress of science have benefited the few at the expense of the many, and to talk of the reign of Queen Victoria as the time when England was truly merry England, when all classes were bound together by brotherly sympathy, when the rich did not grind the faces of the poor, and when the poor did not envy the splendour of the rich.

His prophecies have more than come true. The hundred years that have elapsed since he wrote this notable passage have been the golden age in the improvement of the condition of mankind. Ten or fifteen years have been added to the average life of man. Public health and hygiene have so improved that we take cleanliness and sanitation for granted. Adequate water supply, pure food, clean drains, a sewerage system which has practically destroyed typhoid fever, immeasurably better houses, domestic security backed by an honest and intelligent police, an educational ideal which has given to the average man a degree of knowledge undreamt of a century ago, the substitution for self-help—frequently red in tooth and claw—of a new ideal of responsibility for the weak and unfortunate and aged and unemployed, the cheapening of entertainment, the vast accretion of books and periodicals, the abolition of child labour, the carving out of a new province for law and order by the compulsory fixing of wages and industrial conditions on a civilized basis, the abolition of slavery, the opening of places of power and authority to the man or woman who is rich only in ability, the new conception of the status of women, free speech, religious tolerance—all these and a thousand other things have marked the progress of democracy. No system of tyranny, however benevolent, ever produced so much.

A great legal writer once said that the progress of man was from status to contract. That is a statement worth our reflection. In feudal days everything depended on status: you were a lord of the manor, a freeman, a serf. As was your status, so were your precarious rights. But we, thanks to democracy, live in an age of contract and an age of consent.

The Government orders us, by our consent. Our rights are enforceable, and are not a mere concession by power. Man has not only in the process of evolution stood up in a physical sense, but in the metaphorical sense he has learnt to stand on his own feet. He has become a thing of dignity, a ruler in his own right, a subject of his own will.

That we have all too frequently forgotten the duties which attach to free citizenship cannot be denied. That our system has had its illnesses and that we have been reluctant to probe them to their source is unfortunately true, as I have previously tried to show. But, as we go forward to our great future tasks, we may take courage and resolution from the fact that free self-government has a great history and that what it has done in the past it can, with proper thought and goodwill, do tenfold in the years to come.

It has a great task. I shall speak of it next week.

6 November, 1942.

XXXVI

THE TASK OF DEMOCRACY

IF I were writing a treatise on this great problem I would need to occupy many broadcasts, and your patience, so freely extended to me for nearly a year, would be exhausted. But this will be no treatise. It has been my experience that the most complex problems turn upon one or two pivotal matters, and that once these are understood, question moves rapidly towards answer.

As my previous talks have shown, I, like you, am aware of the weakness of democracy, of its occasional stupidities and shallowness, its temptation to prefer the rabble-rousing spell binder, its habit of giving way to envy, hatred, malice and all uncharitableness. But, giving all this in, I believe in democracy as the only method of government which can produce justice based upon a recognition of enduring human values. The nonsense that is talked, of our choice being between fascism and communism, has never appealed to thoughtful men of our race. For our tradition is of freedom, not of dictatorship—whether the dictatorship be that of one man, a Führer or a Duce, or of what left-wing people, with their passion for long words, call the proletariat. Of us Australian people it will be written, "They were born democrats; as democrats they died."

But democracy's task will not be performed by a race which merely says, "We thank Thee, Lord, that we are not as other men." It will not be performed by men who look complacently at the past and who avoid looking with clear eyes at a troubled future. Our destiny will not be achieved by wordy phrases and empty but resounding promises of a new heaven and a new earth. William Blake, in his famous poem, sung as a hymn in many churches, said:

> I will not cease from mental fight,
>   Nor shall my sword sleep in my hand,
> Till we have built Jerusalem,
>   In England's green and pleasant land.

This is a great verse. It sees that fighting by the sword and fighting by the mind must go side by side. We cannot leave war to the soldiers and the problems of peace to chance. We must think hard if we are not to find that a war has been won and a peace lost.

What, then, must democracy do if it is to be a real force in the new world? In my opinion, two things. It must recapture the vision of the good of man as the purpose of government. And it must restore the authority and prestige of Parliament as the supreme organic expression of self-government. Let me take them in their order.

What is the good of man? This is the oldest of philosophic questions. It admits of a variety of answers. To some advanced political thinkers (I think that is the right expression) it involves making the citizen a pensioner of the State from the cradle to the grave. This is, to adopt a phrase of Mr J. L. Garvin, the very ecstacy of national suicide. I do not want my children and their children to be dependants upon the State: I should much prefer the State to be dependent, to some degree, upon them. The fallacy of this ideal of universal pensioning is that it assumes that the State has unlimited resources which have only to be tapped for all of us to live in ease and comfort for ever. But the State has no resources except those that its citizens create or make available. You cannot have a strong State made up of weak men, or a generous State in which nobody has worked and saved so that there is something to give.

The best and strongest community is not that in which everybody looks to his neighbour hoping for something from him, but that in which every one looks to his neighbour, willing and able to do something for him. In brief, we achieve the good of man when we help and encourage him to be a man—strong, self-reliant, intelligent, independent, sympathethic and generous.

> Teach us the strength that cannot seek,
>   By deed or thought, to hurt the weak;
> That, under Thee, we may possess,
>   Man's strength to succour man's distress.

This means that in the new world we must seek to develop all the intelligence and strength and character in every child. Each one of them must have his chance. We must spend much more on education; we must show that discipline is not the enemy of freedom but its best friend; we must get to know that at least as much genius is to be found and nurtured in Collingwood and Bankstown as in Toorak or Bellevue Hill; that in any event it is better to be a poor man furnished with ability and conscience than to be an advertised member of the "wealthy lower orders". We must train for citizenship. We must alter our standards of value. The Twelve Apostles are amongst the immortals, yet they were poor men as the world calculates wealth.

When the war is won, for every hundred boys and girls who now pass into higher schools and universities there must be a thousand. Lack of money must be no impediment to bright minds. The almost diabolical skill of men's hands in the last forty years must be supplemented by a celestial skill of men's minds and a generosity of men's hearts if we are not to be destroyed by the machines of our creation. In common with other members of Parliament, I must increasingly realize that my constituents are not seventy thousand votes, but seventy thousand men and women for whose welfare and growth I have some responsibility. To develop every human being to his fullest capacity for thought, for action, for sacrifice and for endurance is our major task; and no prejudice, stupidity, selfishness or vested interest must stand in the way.

And to do all this, as a democracy, we must restore to Parliament its authority and responsibility. During 1942 we have been governed by regulations—so far almost five hundred of them—most of them representing the passing will of one or two men. That there must be great executive power in time of war I, as the author of the National Security Act, will be the last to deny. But we must be careful not to slip into the habit of accepting easily and permanently executive legislation.

Parliament is for the time being in the discard. We meet occasionally to pass budgets and estimates; we mildly criticize, and we listen to exhortations; we bow our heads to censorship, hoping that it is all for the best. But parliamentary government is in suspense, and the Executive is in charge; even the law courts inevitably bow to its discretion and judgment.

When the war ends, this too must end. Our rulers must feel the cold wind of public opinion. The minister must cease to be the absolute master and become in truth the servant. Parliament must be recruited from the best we have, and politics once more become a noble and glorious vocation.

There is a quite natural cynicism about these matters which we must overcome. It is dangerous, even though it is quite natural, that we should shrug our shoulders contemptuously when we see the posturing of much-photographed nonentities and listen to the resounding echoes made by tub-thumpers.

The truth is that ever since the wise men gathered about the village tree in the Anglo-Saxon village of early England, the notion of free self-government has run like a thread through our history. The struggle for freedom led an English Parliament to make war on its King and execute him at the seat of government, confined the kingship itself to a parliamentary domain, established the cabinet system and responsibility, set in place the twin foundation stones of the sovereignty of Parliament and the rule of law on which our whole civil edifice is built.

"The sovereignty of Parliament." That is a great phrase and a vital truth. If only we could all understand it to the full, what a change we would make! Sovereignty is the quality of kingship, and democracy brings it to the poor man's door.

Let me end with a note of warning. We must beware of cheap substitutes for the rule of Parliament. We must resist the rule of any sectional body, whether the employers' association or the trades union.

There is some tendency to-day, as there was in the Italy of the early Mussolini, to organize the community by giving to each trade or industry a separate collectivist control of itself through the employers and employees engaged in it. At first sight, this seems reasonable. But second sight will tell us that the most important person is the party of the third part—the member of the general public. He must never surrender his rights. The community is greater than the trade or the business or the craft. There can be no substitute in a democracy for a free and representative Parliament which thinks in broad terms, and makes our own laws for our own purposes as a free people.

13 November, 1942.

XXXVII

THE IMPORTANCE OF CHEERFULNESS

In *Much Ado About Nothing* Shakespeare has a notable passage:

DON PEDRO. In faith, lady, you have a merry heart.
BEATRICE. Yea, my lord; I thank it, poor fool, it keeps on the windy side of care.

A merry heart keeping on the windy side of care—there we have, in a sentence, the importance of cheerfulness.

In the humour of our race there is a great quality—a subtle essence which has its special value at any time, and a superb value in war.

Amid all our troubles and anxieties we must remember how to laugh. Those who tell us not to be optimistic, not to cheer at the news from North Africa, do us a disservice. They are asking us to turn our backs on a great tradition. Cheerfulness is a shining weapon in our national armoury. Hitler and Mussolini have forgotten, if they ever knew, how to laugh. It must be a sad business to be a dictator, anyhow. He has established himself as a superman; he must be maintained as one. Pomp and rhetoric must be his companions. He must not laugh; nor must other people in his presence, for—who knows?—they might be laughing at him. If Mussolini, rehearsing his facial contortions before the mirror, with jutting jaw and blood-charged face, had ever had the wit to laugh at himself, he might to-day be the leader of a happy people and not an object of contempt.

If anybody ever writes a history of the human mind under the strain of war, he will give a chapter of honour to the British people under the blitz. There, he will find few heroics, oddly little black rage, no imitation intellectualism, no showing off. On the contrary, he will find a strange and enduring mixture of brave wit, patient humour, high spirits and merry talk in the midst of dirt and discomfort and danger.

Humour is something about which you cannot argue. We all think we have it, and resent any imputation to the contrary as a deadly and villainous assault. Yet we must admit that humour varies; that there is, to put it generously, one glory of the sun and another of the moon and another of the stars. Take the three peoples from one or more of which most of us have sprung. Scots have a dry, pawky wit, as a rule solemnly pronounced and full of a lingering after-flavour. They have a rare quality of delivering their best shafts at themselves, and are the authors of most of the anti-Scottish tales. The Irish have an iridescent wit, light and buoyant. They have what to many people is an almost incomprehensible quality of being angry and amused at the same thing at the same time. But they do not, as a rule, joke about themselves. The Englishman, to the outsider, is a matter-of-fact, commercial fellow, with an unemotional face and an unadventurous mind. This is a shallow picture. True, he has as a rule very little merely verbal wit, though the moment you say so the ghosts of a dozen Birkenheads will come to vex you. But he has—and I now speak of the average man— a deep, chuckling humour, which is of the very stuff of his character, and one of the secrets of his mastery.

It is, of course, hard to strike an average of any race. British humour ranges from the studied verbal felicities of Oxford and the sharp Cockney repartees of the London cabman to the not always refined stomach comedy of Lancashire. But if the last analysis were made we would, I believe, find in this capacity for making good cheer in the midst of disaster the real explanation for that unpretentious fortitude which has always, in spite of intellectual errors, brought our race to victory.

Let me return to the illustration of the Englishman. It is part of his tradition that he must pretend not to take anything too seriously, not even himself. That is why the French, of whom we do not know very much, since tourist Paris was largely populated by foreigners, have never understood the English; for the French are witty, but not really flippant, and take serious things seriously. They take the Englishman to be a strange and untimely joker whose occasional gravity must therefore be hypocritical. In his latest sketch of his own experiences in France after the outbreak of war, Somerset Maugham refers to the French criticism of the levity, the ribald songs and boisterousness of the British soldiers in France. It was something they found it difficult to understand, for was not war a serious business? Yet you and I, who are of the blood, know that a merry heart goes all the way, and that a man who can jest at danger is the one who is the most likely to see it through.

I was much struck last year by the cheerfulness in the Lancashire aircraft factories. Wherever I went, among people hundreds of whom had in the bombing experienced the sudden arrival of brutal and horrible death in their own homes and streets, I found smiling and determined eyes, and tragedy turned quickly to comedy by some ludicrous story of the blitz.

As General Wavell reminded us in a published lecture on leadership, the Germans, after the last war, set themselves with Teutonic thoroughness to study the reasons for British success. They, so to speak, isolated the humour germ and saw value in it. For all I know, they might have labelled it "Vitamin X". They even attempted to explain and teach it to their young soldiers. In one of their manuals they reproduced Bairnsfather's immortal cartoon of Old Bill and the young recruit in a shell-shattered hut in France. The recruit looks up nervously and says, "What made those holes?" Bill removes his pipe and says, laconically, "Mice". The German editor added a footnote: "It was not mice that made the holes. It was German shells."

These great qualities are part of our own inheritance in Australia. The Italians at Bardia and Tobruk, early last year, may have thought the Australians queer people to march to action singing "The Wizard of Oz". But Bardia and Tobruk were taken.

The Führer of Germany goes to address his people surrounded by guards and bayonets, and the only interruption that is allowed is drilled and disciplined applause. The Prime Minister of Australia has no guard, and his speech is interrupted by the raucous humour of a score of disrespectful interjectors.

The real explanation of the sovereign importance of humour is that it is an individual thing. No Government department regulates or distributes it. It is neither rationalized nor national-ized, nor socialized, nor organized, nor finalized. It is closer to a man than his clothes, for it is a part of him.

No politics based upon gloomy fanaticism can succeed with us, for, to our eternal salvation, we shall always laugh at the wrong time—which will probably turn out to be the right time.

We have proved a hundred times in our history that the strength of a nation is in its individual men and women, and that no formal drill or regimentation can stand against a people who bring to the struggle those unspoiled individual qualities of courage and enterprise and good humour and endurance which are the essence of victory.

20 November, 1942.

www.ingramcontent.com/pod-product-compliance
Lightning Source LLC
Chambersburg PA
CBHW030830020726
47499CB00006B/2139